AF002866

BUREAU

SHORT STORIES

PIECES OF
ARCHITECTURE

Daniel Zamarbide
Galliane Zamarbide
Carine Pimenta

PARK BOOKS

SHORT STORIES

8	I		1995 Tirdad Zolghadr
40	II		EXERCISE Fabrizio Gallanti
74	III		UNTITLED André Tavares
110	IV		AIR THAT MAKES ALL SOLID Zaccharie Lachance
146	V		MILLE IMAGES ET QUELQUES CACTUS A THOUSAND IMAGES AND FEW CACTUS Alexandra Midal
180	VI		FROM GRID TO CLOUD Marina Otero Verzier
219	+ I		ONE MORE SHORT STORY BEFORE YOU GO Daniel Zamarbide
224			BUREAU TALKS 21-12-23 9:37 EST 14:37 GMT
233			INDEX

I
1995
TIRDAD ZOLGHADR

I remember Daniel. I remember him well. We lived in a squat together in downtown Geneva, in the mid-nineties, of which you can see many pictures in this book. Daniel will tell you those are recent work and so on. Towards a Minor Architecture? You bet. Good old Daniel.

Daniel was always a man of many talents, architecture being only one of them. Another talent was that of entering a crowded room and winning you over instantly. The best way to enter a crowded room is to speak loudly as you step inside. Daniel gets it. He really knows how. Got it from architecture school, also known as the Officer's Club. Daniel smiles like he has time on his side. Pas de feu au lac! And his handshake is perfectly firm— even though he's already on to the next guy as he's shaking yours. Then there are the sweeping gestures. Full wide movements of the entire length of his arms. Both arms, preferably.

Look at him. Look at him go. With his pretty eyes, his thick blond eyebrows, his good build and radical hair loss, he has the hesitant charm of a bald pinup. Not bad. A promising young architect with a lingo to match. Lingo? Lingo, yes, lingo. "Towards a Minor Architecture?" That's nothing. From day one, Daniel was happy to insist, for anyone who would listen, that our squat was the Real Thing. A modernist gem in cheap vernacular clothing. A once-in-a-lifetime scoop. Where most of us saw faded paint, rusty frames, routine concrete, weird windows, Daniel saw a walkable jewel. A dance rendered architecture.

The squat really did loom large. You could see it from afar. Twice as wide as it was tall—the proportions of a laptop computer—but perched on dainty V-shaped columns all around. Next thing you noticed were the cacti. Shades of green. Basil and juniper, peppermint and pistachio. I don't believe he included the cacti in this book (though he did include James Last, our beloved pet peacock).

In the evening light, the building would loom larger than ever. Amazing. You like the concrete spleen of Daniel's photos? The saudade of cool cement? Sure you do. No wonder they call modernism an off-shoot of the occult. Few things are more magically attractive to us members of the creative classes. Few things cast a more dramatic shadow over coming generations than concrete slabs and honeycombs, pointing to a seamless planetary future just over the technological horizon. If we no longer care much for universities, or moon colonies, or life on Mars, at least we should care to see what becomes of these concrete contraptions. At least we should imagine them replicated on a mass scale, cantilevered and projected and mushrooming all over the place.

And it was only Daniel who understood this at the time. The rest of us were simply ironic. Nonchalant. Critical. It was the nineties. When we said "architecture," we'd point to ourselves and make a sad face. The same face as when we said "neoliberalism." Or "Venice." (Nothing against Venice! To this day, when we say "Venice," we mean a vernissage, not a city.)

On our very first day at the newly squatted building, Daniel went and built us a shack on the roof for parties and barbecues. People gathered around to watch him sweat and hammer and drag MDF panels across the rooftop. All the while, Daniel went to extraordinary lengths to explain why this structure of his could not in all seriousness be called a "shack." Nor a "cabin" or "shed" for that matter, this being the same kind of violent lunacy as calling the space around it a "rooftop" or the squat itself a "building." Such was the spirit of the age. No terminology was clever enough, ever. The more appropriate terms remained unspecified. But so long as Daniel would sweat and smile in the way that he did, we wouldn't complain.

Pretty soon, the post-"shack" was flanked by outdoor tables. There was a jazzy tune in the background, the volume turned down so low, the mere rustle of a tablecloth would drown it out completely. From here we'd peer down on a lively neighbourhood. The storefronts were stocked by plumbers, butchers, bakers, barbers, electricians, beauticians, tailors, grocers, taquerias and a ballet school. How many square miles still look this way? It's the kind of street that resonates magically with childhood memories, even if you never lived on a street of the kind.

And there we were. Towering above. Basking in the sunshine. We're talking a 1990s kind of sunshine. Again: you can see it in the pictures. High-Res. Shining down on a cushy little offline world. A post–Cold War world. Giddy with the relief of nuclear annihilation postponed. That's the kind of sunshine we're talking about: dare I say a zeitgeistian sunshine through and through. A sunshine that suggests so much to look forward to. Sorry guys. Wish you were there.

Where were we before that squat? In yet another squat. Over on the other side of town. An early colonial apartment block with marble fireplaces. Everybody loved that place. Even the Brigade des Squats—two streetwise cops in jeans and jackets. Even they were congratulatory. Pas mal, pas mal.

It was not to last. But when the bad news finally came, the eviction notice was too civil and courteous to sound like an eviction. It was more like an invitation to a dance—which, in some ways, is precisely what it was. The Brigade des Squats even suggested new downtown options, such as the dance-rendered-architecture that became our next home.

 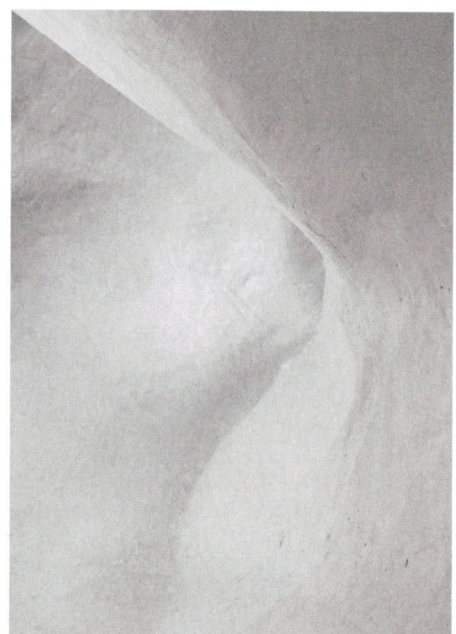

By then, the courtesies and the friendly cops, they had many of us suspicious. Does this stuff qualify as squatting even? A bit too easy, no? The militant types among us, they did not like it. No. They shook their heads: "No." You could see them roll up their issues of *Monde Diplomatique*, tight as a baton or a chicken shawarma, and thump it up and down on the café countertop. Tap tap tap.

DOG GOS GOS

"Come on man. Isn't this a bit too easy? This is no accident. This is a plan. A municipality with no assets, no nothing, nothing at all. But thanks to the squats, it can house people with no housing budget, preserve downtown with no conservation budget, spice things up without immigration. And on top of that. On top of all that. It lays the ground for a whole new ballgame. A gamechanger. Mark my words. From here on out, no bridge or farmyard can just sit there anymore. It needs to be interesting. It needs to be Art and Meaning and World World World. Nothing will be the same again. But for now, here we are. Happily ever after. Living the dream. Win-Win."

Then they'd unfurl the *Monde Diplomatique*, glare at the headlines, sip their lager and nod.

Not that it was all planned out from the get-go. Not really. Does a laboratory need to know exactly what it's doing? Even when it offers hypotheses, conjectures, scenarios, must it offer you an actual road map? Surely no one steers the future as you would a unicycle. What you do have are trials, errors, disappointments — and nice surprises every now and then. In time, the upshot may be Win-Win, lose-lose, or something weirder altogether. A Minor Architecture? Absolutely. Let's make it happen.

I

MAM GOS

II
EXERCISE
Fabrizio Gallanti

I counted fifty images in section 2.
I have been tasked to contribute a text of roughly seven thousand signs. If I divide seven thousand by fifty, each image is accompanied by a caption of precisely 140 signs. The exercise is to write fifty captions each of approximately such length.
Spaces will not be counted.

1
Four steps in some grey matter—concrete or stone. They pivot around a point not in the picture. It takes time for the feet to get used to their rotation and not stumble. (139)

2
Two doors are open, creating symmetry for the camera. It looks like the bow of an ice-breaking ship. The grey floor is the ice. That surface looks cold anyway. (132)

3
All visible surfaces but the floor are coated in plywood. There seems to be a deforming mirror in a round frame reflecting more than just plywood. Or is it a window? (136)

4
Four elongated rectangles, side by side. On the left a niche; the other three are doors. Two of these might open to a closet and the other is a real one. Ideal for hide and seek. (144)

5
We will constantly observe you.
Every three hours a supervisor issues an assessment. After ten consecutive positive assessments, you will be allowed to return to your room. (147)

6
To stay calm, I decided to count all the knots in the wood. Without a pencil or some tape, it turned out to be impossible, as I could not recognize which were counted or not. (141)

7
The glow gently lapping the panelled wall from the right side of the image makes me think that the round shape of image 3 might actually be a real window and not a mirror. (139)

8
Oh gosh, we've run out of grey matter! What shall we do now? They'll kill us! Don't make a fuss, use some plywood instead, we have plenty to spare. Just go by the van and fetch some. (147)

9
The step to access a small alcove looks like a block of pink marble. I wonder whether it is a solid piece of stone or instead just thin slabs surrounding an empty core. (137)

10
He thought that it could be too funny to step on the table and walk over it as in fashion. But he miscalculated the door, bumped into the wall, and fell over the horrified host. (145)

11
The camera seems to have been perched on a very high tripod and carefully centred so that the shadow to the right mirrors the window frame to the left with surgical precision. (146)

12
It would be wonderful if an engine were connected to the light-blue spiral staircase to make it spin very slowly. That would create some sublime disorientation, not too risky. (149)

13
It feels like being in the skull of a medieval knight, glancing at the world through the tiny slit of his helmet. Vegetation is lush, while the brain of the warrior is empty. (144)

14
The socket is perfectly distanced from the two edges of the lower panel. The perfection of that gesture is contradicted by the absence of baseboard: dirt will get there. (143)

15
The grey curve of the veining in the pink marble resembles the tail of a whale plunging into the sea. The whale is afraid of the ice-breaking ship inexorably approaching. (132)

16
The light reveals that the floor is not perfectly polished. There are some slight corrugations—as if it were muddy water, disturbed by something swimming under its surface. (148)

17
The Rorschach effect of two slabs of pink marble cut from the same piece and then juxtaposed side by side recalls the head of an ant or a killer mantis, seen from the front. (142)

18
The pink volume is curved on the ground floor, while a cube on the first floor.
It feels that a very angry giant had pushed a baby's toy into the wrong hole, extruding it down. (144)

19
We are in the freight elevator of some superhero movie, where the protagonist is returning to his den in some industrial loft, ignoring that enemies are hidden there. (141)

20
The pipes elegantly meander over the pink stone, bending when needed. The architect resisted the very British idea of having separate faucets for hot and cold water. (141)

21
There does not seem to be a gash from which to enter the cylinder. Once inside, you are trapped forever, enjoying an eternal shower of warm water, perfumed of shampoo. (140)

22
Using masking tape and a chronometer, one should fix the shape of light over the wood wall to know precisely what figure corresponds to which specific day and time. (138)

23
The curvature of the slab has been calculated by a transport engineer. When the window is open and with appropriate acceleration, take-off is an easy thing to achieve. (142)

24
Barack Obama explained that he used to have dozens of the same blue shirt to avoid overthinking when getting dressed. Light in the closet or drawers becomes superfluous. (144)

25
Is the angle of the rotation between the steps of image 1 the same as the one between the feathers of the peacock's tail? Could these steps close as the tail does? (134)

26
Too many patches of light. Either an LCD projector has been added to the natural light, or the picture is taken behind a window, or someone had too much fun with Photoshop. (143)

27
If you were to race competitively in this pool, what would be the best swimming style? From which end would you dive? Could you flip-turn? And what would be the average lap time? (148)

28
The horizontal opening is wider than a medieval knight's helmet. It looks like the aperture of landing docks in the Star Wars franchise, where starfighters fly in and out. (145)

29
The trees are planted according to a regular grid dimensioned for trucks. They reach the necessary maturity to be felled and turned into paper pulp quite quickly.
(138)

30
There is a filter in the pool that accumulates pine needles and automatically processes them into a perfumed essential oil that is then sold on e-bay for a fortune.
(138)

31
Bacteria in the filter are extremely sensitive. Any chemical disrupts their ability to digest the pine needles. Hence no detergent or soap is allowed when showering.
(142)

32
Inside the hedge, there is a nest of robins. Over generations they have learned the melodies of the music played by the owner of the house, which they sing when he is away. (142)

33
The selection of the stone for the floor was almost painful, because the client wanted a grey that echoed a faint memory of a smoggy day in the Ruhrgebiet of his childhood. (143)

34
No need to move forward. The birds are out there, I can listen to them even through the glass. But there is no way that I can come across that invisible wall.
Now I know. (138)

35
Pacman wanted to gobble all the landscape. But his dietologist insisted that he had to lose the round shape and become angular before changing habits. He obliged. (138)

36
In the woods, one is perplexed whether to look down or not. It helps to avoid stumbling on a root or stepping on a snake, but then it is disappointing to see a paper tissue or a can of beer. (153)

37
Mickey Mouse started doing crystal meth. He has become very skinny, and he is always on the hunt for a new fix. When he is in need, he can be extremely aggressive. (134)

38
I wonder how much larger the leaf extends beyond the limits of the cropped frame. I would be upset if I discovered that just a few millimetres were left out. It would feel lazy. (146)

PAN   PAN

39
While the architect was talking with the contractor, the workers were laughing about his obsession with the concrete moulding. "Why, to make shadows for ants?" (137)

40
The smell of the beeswax reminded her of the massive, very polished oak desk of the notary who very solemnly read her father's will to her and her siblings. (130)

41
He waited, every day at five sharp, for a motorboat passing on the lake in front of the window. It was always the same slender girl with black hair and a red swimsuit water-skiing. (149)

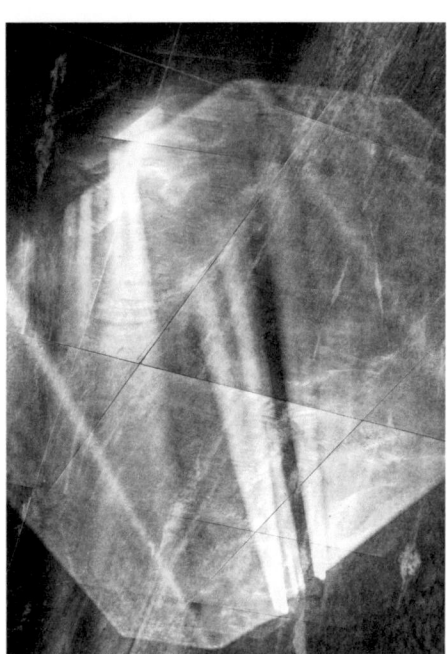

42
When he was a kid, his uncle gave him a kaleidoscope. He always brought it with him, wherever he went, to look through it. One day, a school bully stepped on it, crushing it. (143)

43
The family stopped paying the cemetery fee when they went broke. The management then auctioned off the niche's very beautiful sculptures, leaving it desolately empty. (144)

44
In the dead of night, the tiny train station café was the only place to find a living soul in town. The owner made the place a secure port for everyone lost and alone. (136)

45
These two curved shapes draw a complete blank. In this picture the drive towards "non-referential architecture" has perhaps reached its point of no return. (134)

46
Sometimes they shared the same eerie feeling of just being guinea pigs in a terrarium, under the constant monitoring of some crazy, malevolent scientist. (132)

BBB

DOG

CDM   FLY

47
Is there a logic for spiral staircases—clockwise or counter-clockwise? Is it like water in sinkholes, turning in opposite directions north or south of the equator? (141)

48
The stems on the right could be pipes descending through the floor, a very stylized Christmas tree, or an over-designed coat rack that will damage any garment placed on it. (145)

49
The sofa seems to be waiting for David Lynch to be seated on it, his legs crossed, elegantly yet casually dressed. A very mellow voice asks him some profound questions. (141)

II

50
I would not be afraid of falling. Otherwise, I am sure that I would let something drop, bounce on a step, and then have to spend a long time four-legged on the floor looking for it. (148)

III
UNTITLED
André Tavares

1
Fog has the privileged effect of blurring forms. When over snow, its fluid shapes make it difficult for the eye to focus. Air and soil are brought together in a mixture of concrete suggestions and volatile glimpses. There are no boundaries. For seconds everything is clear.

Amidst the fog we can find an inhabited stone. It defies conventions, it needs to do so. Inhabiting the mountain is not necessarily for urban users. Yet, the photography blurs its boundaries until we lose track. What is the materiality of the rock? Are we lost in the mountain?

Once inside, neatly trimmed wooden furniture can restore us to a conventional world. We only find ourselves many pages further on, the wooden tones of the pages contrasting with the flourishing green that will follow.

The fences help to build a repetitive grid. It is endless, seamless, without boundaries. There is no beginning and no end, and yet it moves from white to black to green to blue. We are within ideas, conveying the expectations of architects striving to create spaces. Atmospheres are compelling, but blurriness seems to challenge construction and materiality.

I recall the mushrooms. They grow by themselves, as the ice melts and creates stalactites. We expect nature to generate the powerful green hues that coloured the pond, the canal, the forms that make the garden so special. The wall is completely fake; it looks like an abandoned house, but it isn't. It was built from scratch to look as if it was already there. And it hides the bold concrete structure that shapes the monumental micro house. Everything seems the opposite of what it should be. Yet the mushrooms keep on growing. Four stacked arched windows seem to be out of scale, but their circular geometry rebounds on the forms that follow. The window frame opens and its geometry brings a dynamic quality to the frame, its shade collapsing on the next page. If there was a breeze coming through, it might activate the windmill to produce energy for the mysterious pyramidal shape over the desert. Were the windows in the desert? The harshness of the shadows, so different from the blurry fog, might suggest the location.

The folded metal sheets protect something we do not know. The cone rises together with the light pyramid and the folded inner mystery. There is no fog, but the mystery remains.

DOG　　　　　　　　　　　　　　　　　　EAU

EAU

OAK   EAU

EAU DOG

2
Wood, wood, wood. We are inside. The house archetype is still here, entangled with drawers, doors, and spaces hidden behind. We must discover them. The wood can be smooth, immaculate, but it is an industrial product. Out of the factory, unlike the fog and like the metal sheets we have encountered. There is also a different wood, with knots, revealing its natural source: "Once I was a tree." Everything is what it is: fog is water, wood confirms it is not a digital product.

The geometries are intersected with curves. Suddenly we are no longer in cosy interiors but in larger spaces. Are they the same? The bold cantilever highlights the landscape. There will be beauty. But the concrete does not have the fresh, acrid scent of nasty concrete. There is no one on the building site. Concrete is an artificial stone, but the stone is real, perfectly cut, with lavish surfaces whose patterns recall the millennia of its formation. Round, prismatic—the angles keep on colliding.

And we find that the green and the animals, clothed as buildings, also strive for beauty. It is not a textile beauty, but organic matter looking to where it should move. The leaves, the concrete, the forest. The swimming pool reminds us how strange everything is. Will the peacock meet the cat swimming for a morning record? How fresh is the summer water? How warm is the winter water? How pleasing can pleasure be?

We go back to geometry. Hexagons, circles, spirals, curves, countering shapes, slicing forms. Is concrete as subtle as the morning light? Is marble really opaque? Or does beauty bend smoothly?

Do not go outside, it was just a glimpse. Far away, in the landscape, we can imagine that a world exists. But do we really want to be there? The city has no pine trees, no sensitive fluids, just harsh smells and sweat. Even if the spaces are not yet inhabited, we have to keep the mystery. It is the only way to imagine a different city, a space where our imagination can be built. How is it built?

EAU　　　　　　　　　　　　BAG

AFR

BAG

3
We finally meet the flowers, the water, and the sun. We long for the bees, for cross-pollination, for love and beasts copulating, for some harshness. It is there. Vegetation hides biodiversity: there are no mushrooms without wild boars, spiders, mosquitoes, unpleasant bites, and pleasant sensations. Where are we? This is not a digital world. Every bit of marble, every crack in the concrete, every reflection in the glass—it is not a deceptive game of illusions. Where are we?

Architecture inhabits the realm of ideas. That is where we brought it, for better or for worse. But ideas are more powerful when real, when their weight can be measured. Impact is a funny word, and architecture has impact. Often it is not funny, it is simply work. To work is to build—with materials. Materials are beyond ideas, and to change ideas one needs to change materials.

While ideas need reality to become dreams, images need dreams to become reality. The worm might find the bird, the house will be dusty, the tree will become the hut, the hut the bird cage. Everything will become something else. Hence, the rhythmic repetition of industrial control flirts with the rough uncertainty of wood barbs, copper pipes within intricate geometries. We can go up but we must come down.

And we reach the city, it was inevitable. No matter the entrance doors, the neon signs, the lush panoply of sounds we can't hear. The cargo has arrived and totemic forms are there not to be celebrated but to become city instead, to be inhabited. Long live the flowers, the colours of the rainbow, the birds in the sky.

FLY FLY

MIG	EAU

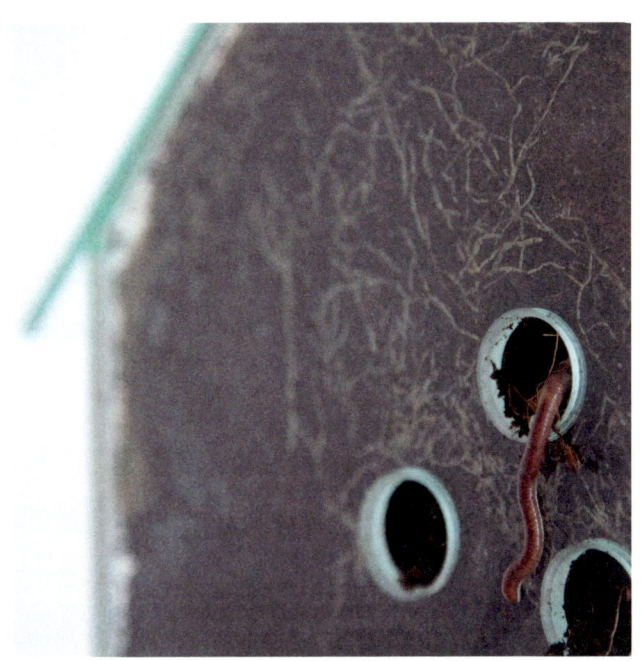

4

In a perfect world, things should be as we like them. Needless to say, they are not. We can try to build with mushrooms, design shelters defying nature, create ponds with mysterious and powerful colours. Yet, people continue to walk desperately outside in the street. It is cold outside, it is not late but the day is gloomy and it will soon be night. The red lights of cars braking lend the streets a familiar atmosphere. The book calls for an eminent contrast between what architects expect and what happens outside.

Let's start with the images. We get that several projects are blending into rhythmic sequences. These sequences are beyond the original practices, they are not explanatory, they bend the sources to a novel hypothesis: the book will be something else. Shall we forget the original constructs, abandon their purposes, desires, and achievements and focus on the visual apparatus their images produce? Or shall we decorticate the hints and attempt to reach their original contexts? With the resources we have, the latter question is impossible to answer. No way we will ever understand. That's exactly the fun of it: we can make whatever we want with the built ideas.

Architecture is the result of human labour. Isn't it?

THE BAG　　　　　　TOM

III

The light floods the room from above, taking advantage of the reflective whitish varnishes. The upper area is plastered, contrasting textures in different shades of white. The yellowish upper corner counters the bluish background, subtleties that the strong *monstera* highlights. The geometrical forms emerge from the dark background. The strong beam backlights the structure, vertical and horizontal steel bars shaping a perfect scenario for a techno sound explosion. There is a cascade of tiles, not a staircase but a sequence in dialogue with the pictorial framing. The overlapping colours seem to fade into the wall. The forms emerge from the dark background. Or was it the other way around?

Pink and green, horizontal and vertical, foreground and background. Then suddenly the library shelves bring randomness to the contrasting actions. A book is a book, and its industrial nature is not amenable to careful arrangement. Libraries and bookshelves are easy to set up but hard to read. That's why the steel structural profile is such a good match with the ceramic tile, and the books, although gentle and promising, are just books.

The brick wasn't there. He searched. That nobody noticed its absence was a mystery to him—he was used to the building site. He knew the unique perfume of fresh cement, but he was finding flowers and bees instead. Not erotic orchids, but lavish leaves of green gradients. And delicate blossoms. After a while he gave up. They were enjoying the music, its steady sound bites and magnetic reverberations.

5
The cart was sliding down the roller coaster. Nobody was screaming, but he sensed the feelings, experiences, tastes, colours, and love and everything else. While sliding down, he thought: who the hell did it? The cart flipped into another unexpected acrobatic move, and he remembered things he had read. The hand had power over capital, which meant that the worker could claim his rights simply because he had the knowledge to make things happen. With a hammer in his hand, he could knock in a nail; nobody hammered in nails the way he did. He felt confused and dizzy— the vapours and rhythms were puzzling and there seemed to be no way out. A grid of tiles, twenty by twenty.

BG1 BAS

III

CCS　　　　　　　　　　　　　　TOM

AG2　　　　　　　　　　　　　　　　　　　　　　BG1

BG1 MUR AG1

BG1

CDM

IV
AIR THAT MAKES ALL SOLID
Zaccharie Lachance

I wonder why Bureau takes so much effort to blur everything. Architecture as I have known it is always quite direct in its representations. Why is it so complicated to just make architecture, develop projects and present them like everyone else—in images of what's going on in the studio, in plans, sections, renderings, and photographs or films of completed works?

Going through the book they presented me, I ask myself: why this sense of evaporation, as if they wanted to avoid being solid, being physically present? They seem to partner with a photographer very much in the "hazy mood," one that avoids showing "real" architectural elements.

Is this part of the practice's agenda? Do they really try to escape from the hard reality of their material, concrete, tough, and down-to-earth profession? Why such effort to show the poetics, the airy lines of beautifully rendered environments, through photography? Isn't it a bit exasperating, all this hazy beauty? It feels like slippery terrain, but since I'm writing this carte blanche, it seemed to me I should spend a little more time on the images, the main support for this text, even as I also know the work and have visited and experienced some of it.

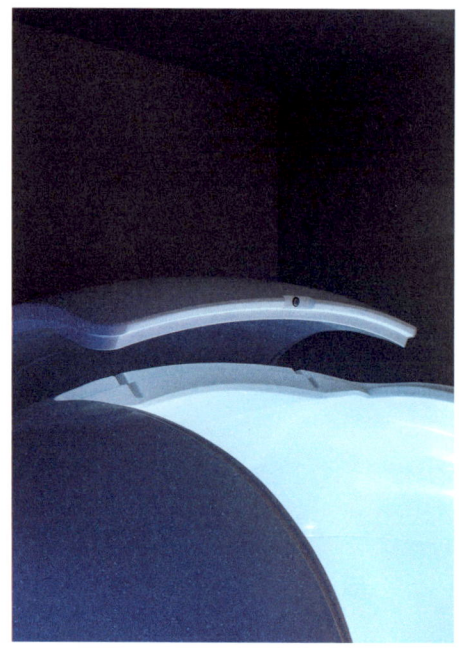

IV

I ran from the world of architecture quite early in my career, not finding much of what I dreamed of as a student. Pursuing architecture, I stumbled upon a very stiff profession, one that shines as experimental but that ends up running after ambition, notoriety and innovation—money and fame, in other words. I suppose I did not find the right people or contexts. In any case, this is most probably the reason why Bureau approached me for this brief writing, something I had not done for a while.

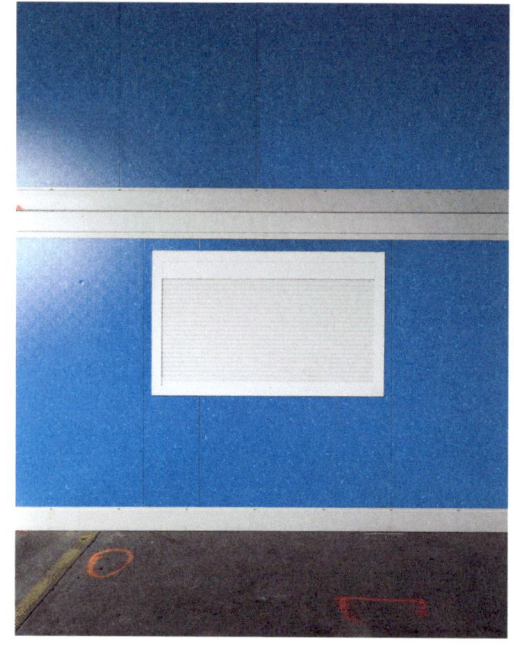

Analyzing the work from the perspective of more conventional modes of architectural representation, I quite quickly reach an early conclusion: there is a sense of opacity on what is shown. What seems to be hidden are the recipes, the secret ingredients, the works in progress, the tools, the ongoing material. What is proposed is what has become solid, built, installed, made, lived. Very rarely is it a virtual image, a rendering; even the very thing that architects spend most of their time on—drawings—are absent.

Is this an intentional move against the material opulence of the early 2000s? Remember *Content* at the Neue Nationalgalerie, in 2004? Or *Archaeology of the Minds* at the CCA in 2002?

IV

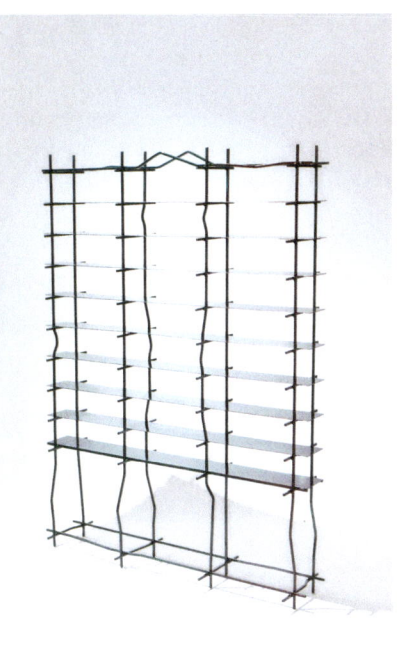
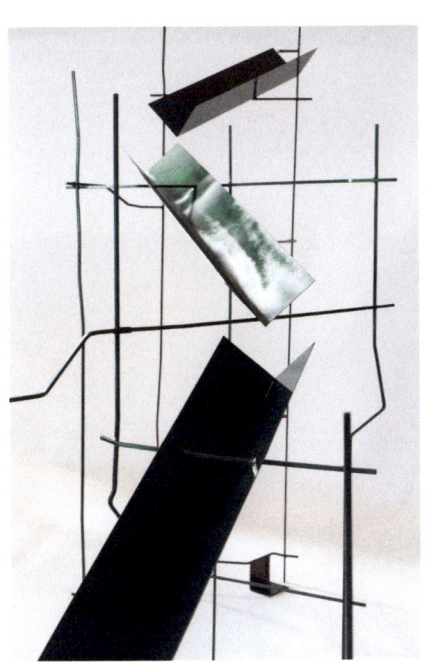

IV

By some strange coincidence, I happened to see those two exhibitions as a kid, holding my parents' hands. I was just a young teen at the time and was there to accompany their passion for architecture. The former, in Berlin, left a fantastic impression on me—a fabulous punk playground, perfect for my constrained teenage culture. Both featured models by the dozens or hundreds—variations and iterations and exploded wunderkammers ripped from the studios of the two of the most important rivals at the time: OMA and Herzog & de Meuron. This moment of architectural history opened the doors to the invasion of blue and pink Styrofoam in architectural studios. Those who could afford it and related more to the Swiss took it further and made beautiful studio objects—wood and metal pieces, neatly crafted; the rest, those who enjoyed the attractive and "dirty" attitude of the Dutch, kept with foam and the beautiful Proxxon hotwire cutter.

Architecture is slow and, most of the time, architects are not immersed in a creative everyday life. The work is more about emails and meetings like many other professions, with some moments to sketch here or there. Maybe this is the one reason they keep so much material around, so they can be surrounded by something that might resemble an artist's studio. But they are not artists: they mostly react to commissions—briefs, in most cases. No one would come to the studio every morning to "practice" if there were no contracts with clients who need architecture for one reason or another. The bigger the studio, we could say, the further the principals are from creative activities, and so the more material they need around.

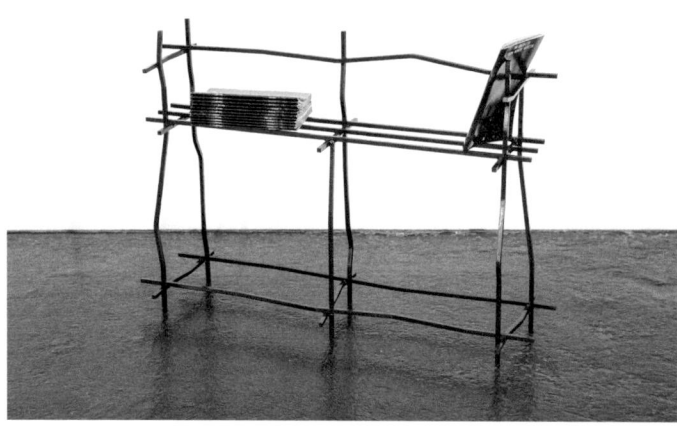

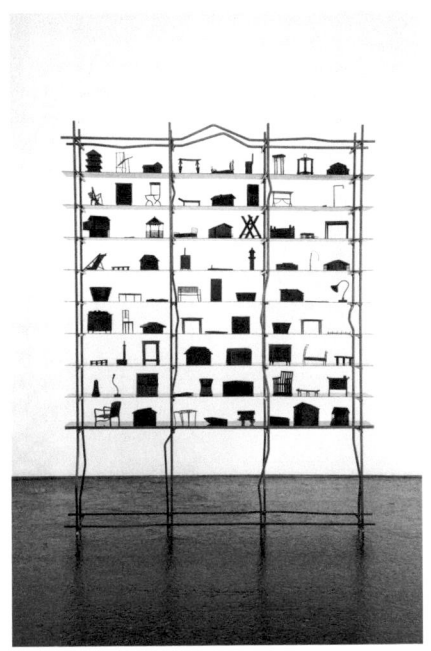

MON OAK

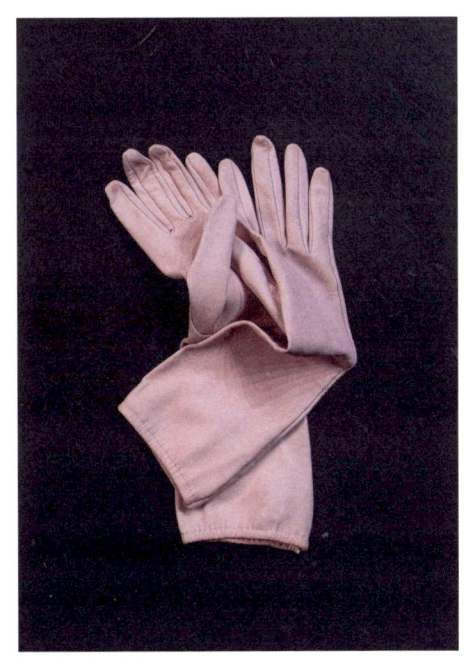

In *Content*, junk is extremely material: there was no blurriness. And the contrast might be telling, between that specific moment and the next decades of OMA's built work, which did not seem as explosive and pornographic as the *Content* exhibition catalogue.

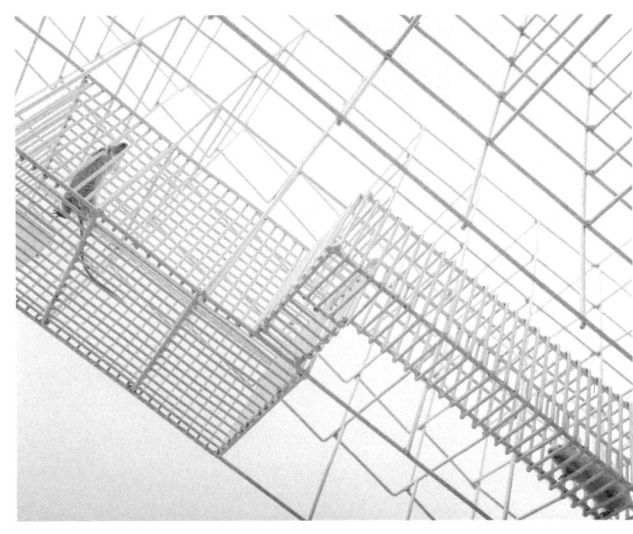

I know for a fact that the work of OMA (written, built, and exhibitionary) was, at least at one point in time, an important influence for Bureau. And I thus wonder if they are not working in response to the 2000s, trying to do the inverse of OMA by making ungraspable images of completed work. Instead of undressing the office, they seem to do the opposite, maintaining a distance between completed work and how all of it is made.

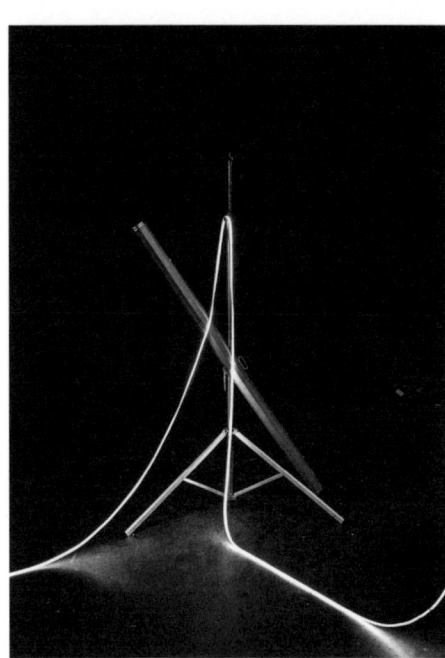

On the one hand, this attitude can be perceived as a form of arrogance or distance. On the other, it preserves a sort of domestic privacy—a cultural reaction to the rather common mode of revealing as much as possible or creating as many images as possible to keep the world's attention.

Obviously, there's the name and its absurdly generic defiance: Bureau, but of what, exactly? The office clearly seems to want to hide, to slip from clear definitions. Their work thus raises continuous questions. Does the name reflect a lack of courage? Is it a way to avoid confrontation with what is conventionally considered a more real world? Or is the magic "box" of Bureau always ready to surprise with unexpected games? Hard to say.

IV

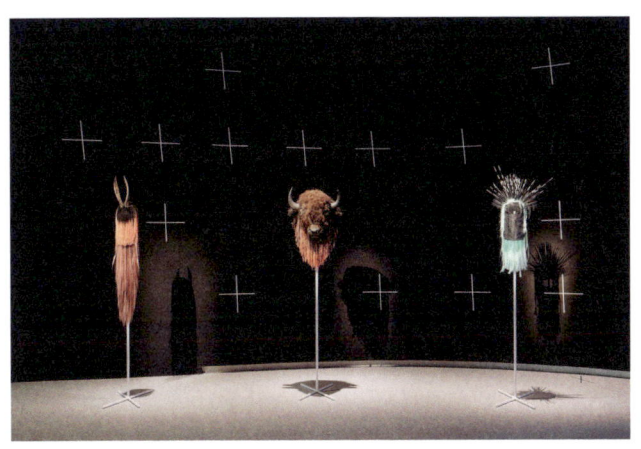

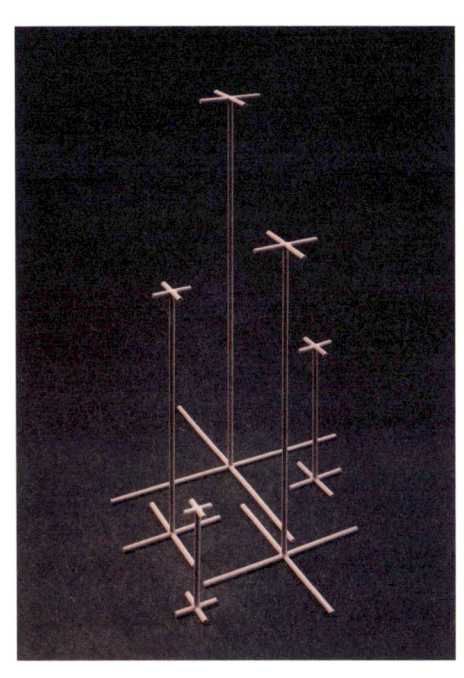

But there is something intriguing in showing architecture as a multiplicity of situations. Their use of photography, inevitably documentary in that it uses physical reality as a point of departure, could be revealing just that fact. Architecture—Bureau's architecture specifically—is just part of something else, composed of fragmented moments, smaller or bigger stories, supports of experiences that have been, are being or will be lived in the environments the photographs show.
I suspect some kind of escape from a state of completeness. As much as the work seems neat or precise, it does not want to present as a whole but rather as pieces of larger stories.

IV

ROG ROG BG1

This strategy, whether purposeful or not, says something about more recent architectural thinking. Architecture now is not only about building buildings but about pieces and conversations within a diversity of situations. And so it goes for Bureau, staying with the trouble of incomplete works. Through their insistence on fragments, they seem to have no need to actually achieve a visible built work, as they embrace every space they can to fabricate and play around fragmental conditions. And it seems to be satisfying for them, enough to keep going with the practice. This attitude takes them to stage design, to texts and short movies, to design pieces and gardens, interiors and publics spaces—anywhere where a discussion is possible, no matter the architectural format.

IV

DIN

CIR

Is this attitude durable? After ten years of existence, do Bureau feel the need to reach a next step, to grow up, to become more stable or more solid, to have a more substantial portfolio of built objects? Or will they continue to expand in puzzle pieces that will never come together as a whole? Or will they, at one point, like I did, see the limitation of that experimental "fooling around" and join me at the Audet cattle farm in Charlevoix? If they need, I know the boss. We are hiring.

V
MILLE IMAGES ET QUELQUES CACTUS
A THOUSAND IMAGES AND FEW CACTUS
Alexandra Midal

Voulez-vous vous laisser conduire au bord d'un lac des Alpes ? Le ciel est bleu, l'eau verte, tout repose dans une paix profonde.

Pour ma part, je suis fier de constater que mes intérieurs ne produisent aucun effet en photographie (...)

Adolf Loos, "Architecture," 1910

On August 11, 2022, Bureau invited me to react to a series of images spread over several pages. The only key was an extract from *Mille Plateaux* by Gilles Deleuze and Félix Guattari. The sole clue: the images were interwoven associations between Bureau and me. Great. I've been following the effervescent Bureau with interest for a long time. Their projects resonate with me. The selection of pages I received invisibly connect images to one another, surrendering to my interpretations, allowing meaning to emerge from the interstices left between each of them, inviting me to make free associations through anadiplosis. These principles of analogy reproduce the cervical patterns of information distribution engaged by our synapses, and I wonder what these enigmatic visuals mean: what narratives are they intended for? What stories are there to guess? What is Bureau playing at with this fragmented puzzle?

Storytelling: by taking up Michel de Certeau's concept of the gap and revisiting the displacement towards territories in images, Bureau places itself on the margins of the institution and frees up a point of view that gives rise to new interpretations, defying the usual order of things according to which, by convention, an image should illustrate a project. Here, it's the only trace. My task, then, should I choose to accept it, as stated in the credits of this famous spy series and franchise, is to take over this rebus punctuated here and there by heterogeneous elements: flora, a horse, neon lights, materials, walls, models, etc. But to do what with it? Is it an impossible mission to understand these photographs of landscapes, vegetation, plants and cacti, whose presence has been so frequently associated with "visions," "addictions," and other "psychotic pleasure centers of the brain," as Reyner Banham has called them? Far removed from the imagination of the Wild West and its gold-hungry colonizers, cacti are curiosities whose vertical presence interrupts the horizontality of the lake in my Franco-Swiss daily life, so well described by Adolf Loos in the preamble to my remarks. How can I, who has been wandering through this image cryptography for almost two years, without instructions or captions, decode all this? How can I get a rabbit out of this visual script?

Inhabiting the space of the book page in this way turns Bureau away from any functionalist architectural origins, replacing them with the power of mystery and emotion. Oscillating between fantasy and strangeness, the page distills the scattered pieces of a fascinating puzzle. It was from this angle, following the explosion of mechanization shaken by the industrial revolution and its criteria of technological standardization and planning archetypes, that modernity had dreamed of a new individual, modern and intensely psychological, able to redraw their links with the fragmented space of his environment as well as their psyche. Isn't my soul just as dispersed today in the hyper-individual age of late capitalism?

V

BUR   ANT   BAG

This perspective was undoubtedly clearer during the heyday of horror cinema in the 1920s, when images were able to crystallize and engender states of mind through architectural embodiments that, better than any other art form, were able to condense the dramatic tension of narratives—catalyzing, both psychologically and symbolically, the characters of cinematic fiction. Architecture became the central axis of the genre: like a living being, emotionally innervated, the papier-mâché house exposed itself until it reached paroxysmal states. As a Gothic lair of torment resonating with the soul, the psycho-aesthetic dimension of these pages in turn accommodates psychological underpinnings. But make no mistake: this notion is not a thing of the past, and something is at work behind the apparent calm of the images, behind the aligned plants and the horizontality of the lake. I come face to face with the discreet presence of spectres and ghosts linked to hidden energies and forces. Everywhere, the supernatural reigns. Astonishment! Hard to swallow this revelation. I fear that Bureau has taken possession of my soul and is manipulating my perceptions...

What if, following the example of Psychodiagnotic, the famous personality test invented by Swiss psychiatrist Hermann Rorschach (1921) and designed to determine personality based on the interpretation of ten ink-stained boards, Bureau is encouraging me to formulate mental projections in images that they would then print? What use can I be to them? Perhaps the answer lies in the process described by writer Serge Brussolo in *Aussi lourd que le vent* (1981). Brussolo stages a protocol for building architecture by hardening rare gases with a sound frequency. He describes how, using a solution that modifies the frequency of the voice, his characters create vocal sculptures: by combining sounds and insults, they form fugitive, ghostly edifices. Are thoughts delicately laid down on the paper of this work?

Since the nineteenth century, the emergence of ghost stories has frequently been associated with a complex, if not conflicting, relationship with technology. Spectres have been seen as betraying the incomprehensible and disquieting nature of existing technology. Bureau revisits the apparent calm of surfaces through photographs that better conceal their invisible project. As a result, as with Brussolo's ephemeral buildings, we're left with a stark observation! If nothing really exists at Bureau other than the images you're holding in your hands; if their buildings are nothing more than elegant glossy pseudo-productions; if their projects are nothing more than rumours, these architecture-visuals serve to protect them from commercial speculation and allow them to foment another project. In Poltergeist, Bureau embodies a haunting, that natural force of the mind, ready to seize joyfully upon you, the reader, who is reading this book from the comfort of your armchair at home, and their plans will remain secret for a long while.

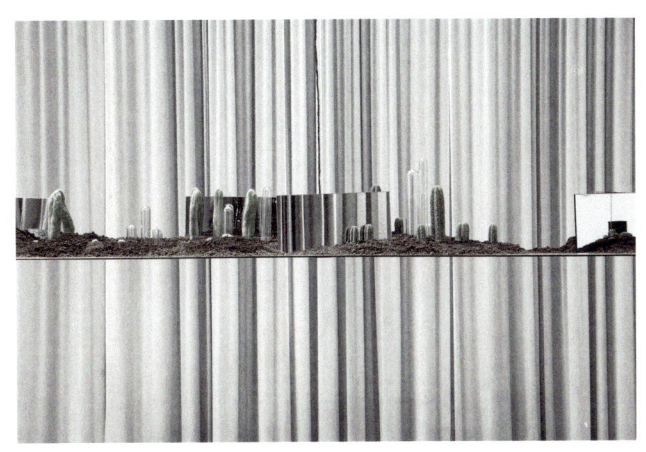

MON LAM KLB 163

CIR CCS

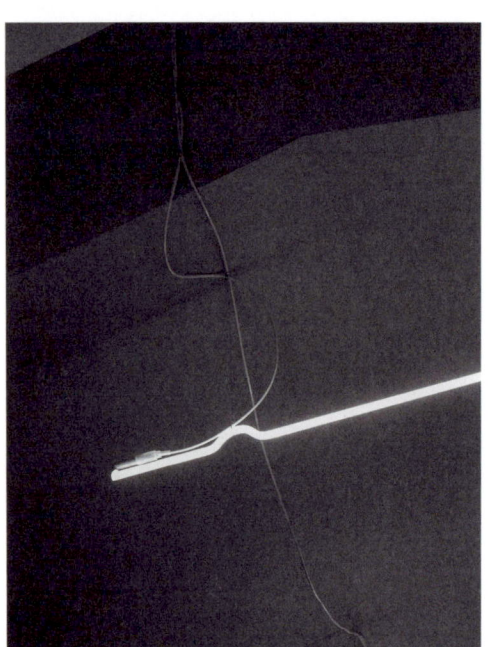 

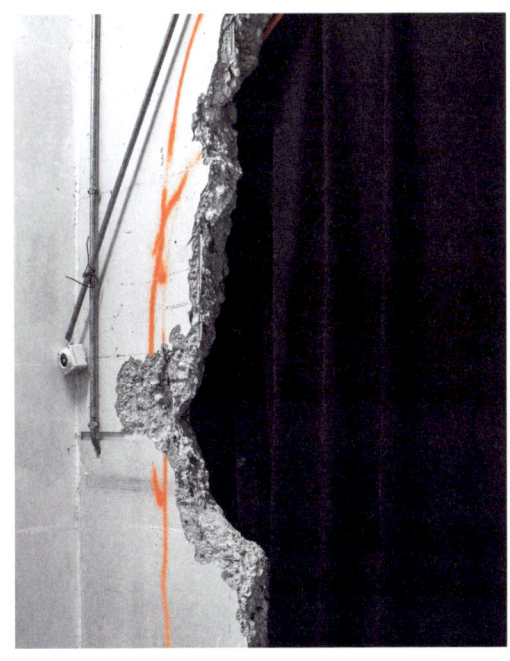

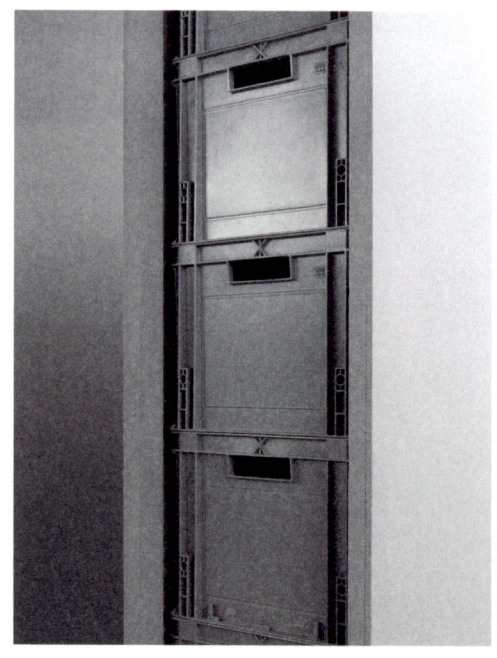

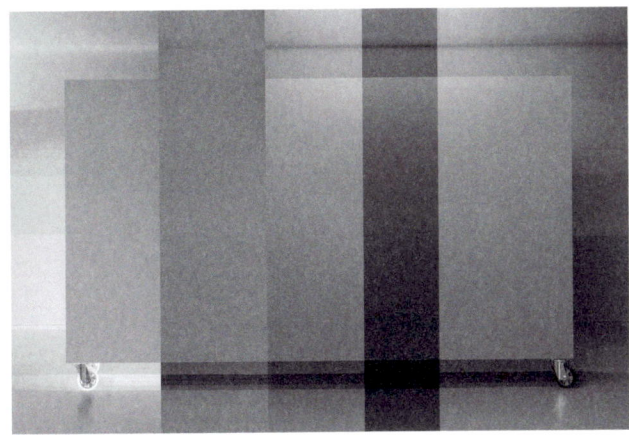

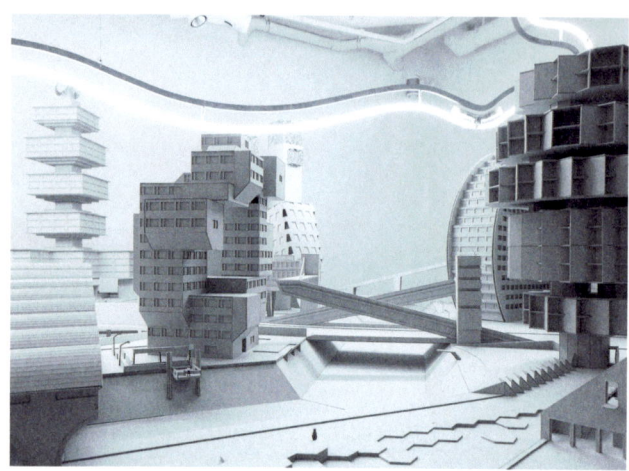

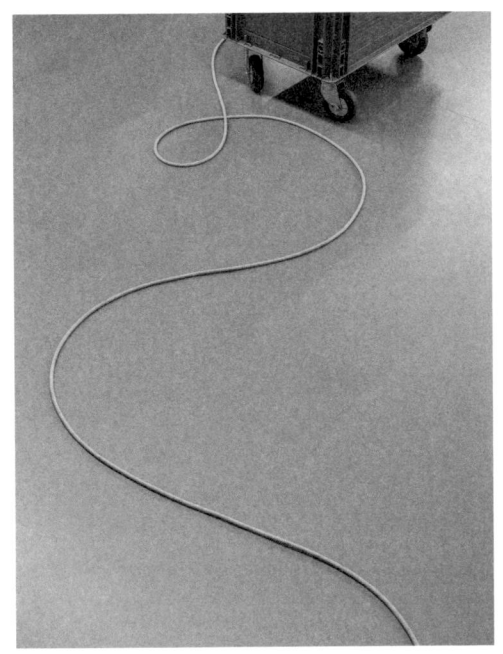

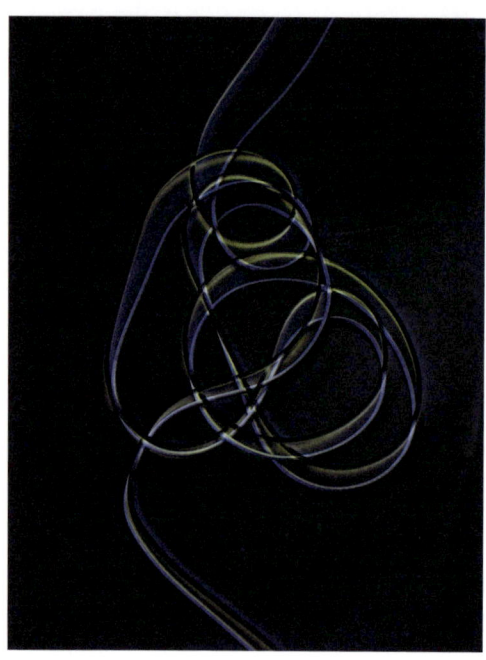

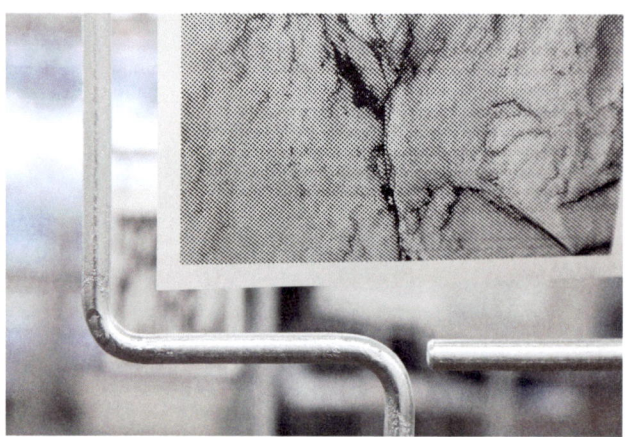

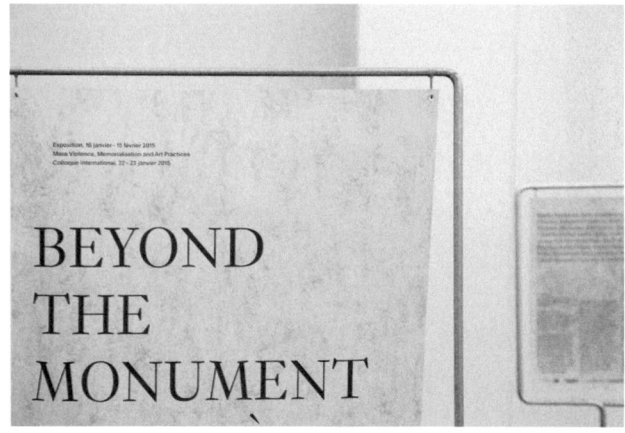

VI
FROM GRID TO CLOUD
Marina Otero Verzier

I am about to tell a story. It is the story of a grid who wanted to become a cloud. It is in fact the story of architecture.

I want to dismantle all grids, one after the other. In the grid, we are captive of the fear to the unknown. The grid rationalizes, organizes laying regular lines. The grid designs—is in itself tantamount to design, to architectural design. Architects love it. So do managers and engineers.

The grid, the Cartesian grid, serves to draw, calculate, optimize, standardize, replicate, and ultimately control space. The grid's abstract aesthetic stimulates the human's crudest ambitions—dreams of mastery of space and time, of territory and resources —ambitions that drove the mechanical age and the formation of capitalism, that instigated economic efficacy at the expense of ethical and ecological awareness.

The grid is, above all, a conceptual speculation, writes Rem Koolhaas in *Delirious New York*: "in its indifference to topography, to what exists, it claims the superiority of mental construction over reality. Through the plotting of its streets and blocks it announces that the subjugation, if not obliteration, of nature is its true ambition."

The grid is the blueprint of colonial plantations and cash books, the base of spreadsheet architectures. It grows data centres. It organizes the world's driest desert in colourful lithium ponds, where millions of litres of water are evaporated every day in the name of powering the system.

The grid supports extractivism.
It constructs distinctions and categories that delineate what is alive and what is lifeless. It sees commodities where there is matter. It sees nonlife instead of living ecosystems.

The grid legitimized Western man's domination of landscape, resources, and other beings. It embodies speciesism. It sells the human as a unique and superior being. It defines and discriminates entities, bodies, and identities. In measuring bodies against an imagined normative one, the grid genders and racializes.

VI

PAN   DOG

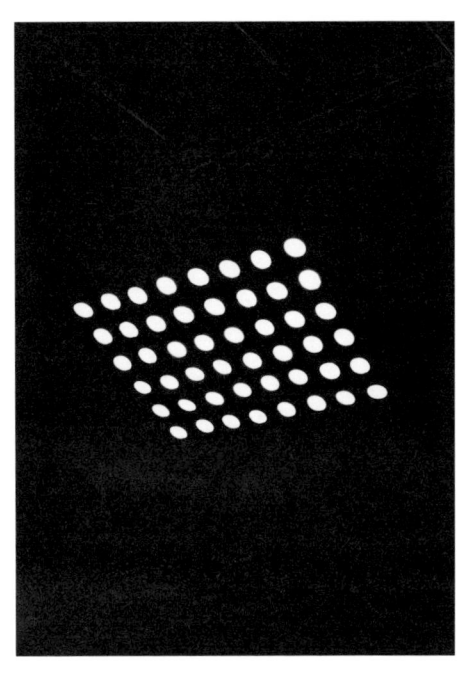

DOG LAM 185

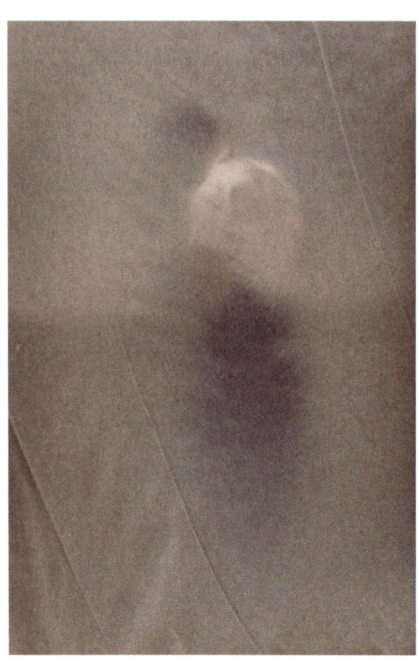

MUR AG2

In *A Casa*, Madelon Vriesendorp depicts the Statue of Liberty about to go to bed, tearing apart an armature of geometric skin to uncover a naked body.

The grid's bare assertive lines define insides, outsides, ups and downs. They produce differential social spaces, spaces that facilitate and prevent the encounter and movement of bodies.

The grid encloses space. It validates the ridiculous idea that someone can actually own space. It proclaims logic and science, yet it is in fact an act of faith, a work of fiction.

VI

The grid is "antinatural, antimimetic, anti-real," writes Rosalind Krauss in "Grids." The grid is "what art looks like when it turns its back on nature." In the flatness that results from its coordinates, the grid is the means of crowding out the dimensions of the real and replacing them with the lateral spread of a single surface."

The grid is ubiquitous. It permeates interiors and exteriors. When you no longer see it, it is because it grew inside, aided by fertilizers and by antidepressants. From the inner, it creates the illusion of order and legibility, an inevitable aesthetic and repressive experience, an ontological version of the world so perfected that it seems inevitable.

Isn't it beautiful, the grid?

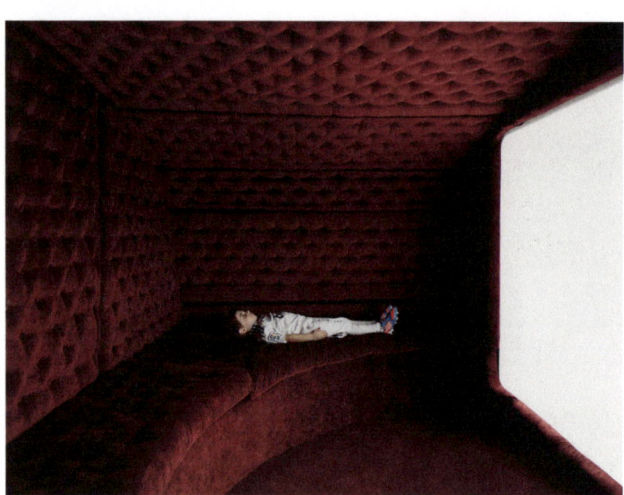

The grid occurred to Superstudio when they went looking for a "skinless" architecture, "an architecture in which the outside arises from the inside, straight out of the inner life of the men who live in it," one that could "put cosmic order on earth," that instead of subjugating, could embolden nature. The grid then expanded over the entire world until it reached its end.

Where Superstudio draw an endless grid,
I offer a cloud.

The cloud is contrary to the compartmentalized world of the grid. It is not made of 0s and 1s. It is low-definition, indeterminate. And yet, it is capable of dismantling the boundaries that enclose the world—capable of opening up previously inconceivable futures.

VI

KLB   TOM   SWS

The cloud, this cloud, questions modernity. It challenges how modernity educates us to know and describe the world. It invites immeasurability and exceeds categories. It is non-Cartesian. It is difficult to describe under dualist categories.

BAG AFR

The cloud grows unpredictable environments and relations between space, matter, and organisms. It morphs slowly and melts platonic solids, geometries. The cloud's vaporous borders make it difficult to draw a line between inside and outside. It makes everything equally important—or unimportant.

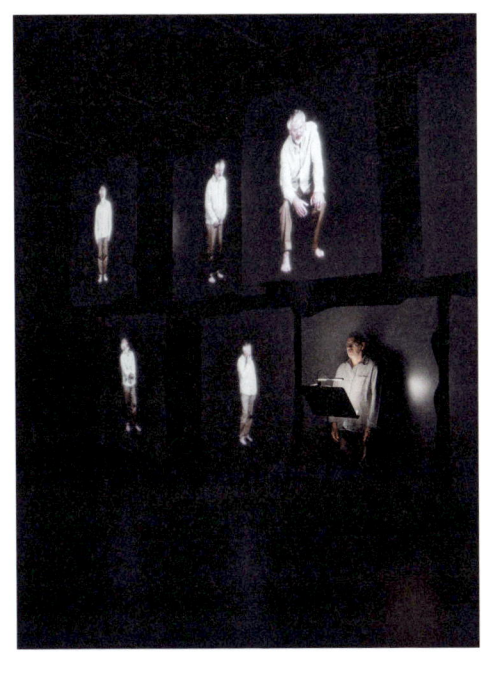

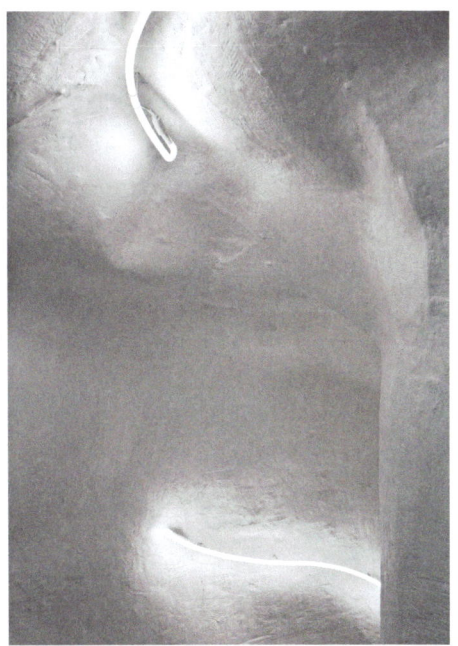

Though both alive and able to itself give life, this cloud is not here to communicate the divine. It celebrates the erotic dimension of the body, its emancipatory role. It is the catalyst of dynamic interconnected worlds that exist in the seemingly banal act of breathing.

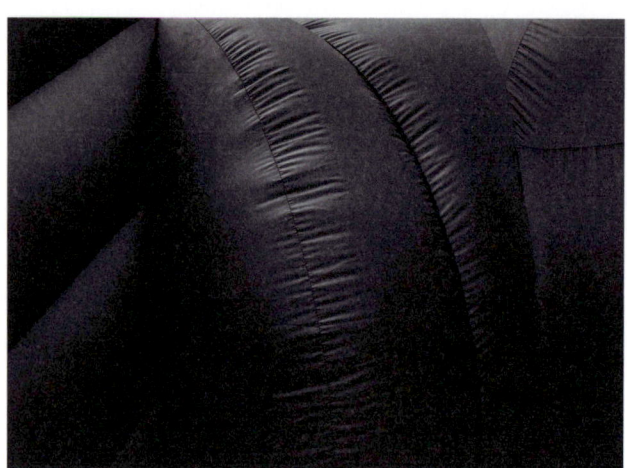

The cloud is a political space that allows
us to be breathed in and to breathe.
In the cloud we find and inhale each other.
The cloud is porosity and interdependency
between bodies and the atmosphere,
between bodies and the environment.

"Before every utterance on earth, there is a cloud, an almost immobile air," writes Luce Irigaray in *To Be Two.* "The plants already breathe, while we still ask ourselves how to speak to each other, without taking breath away from them."

The cloud is a non-disciplined architecture. It asks if the architectural canon could be put aside. It doesn't suggest it has to be erased or forgotten—just perhaps acknowledged as serving interests that are no longer pertinent, too often constructed by means that are not only outdated, but no longer ethically and ecologically tolerable.

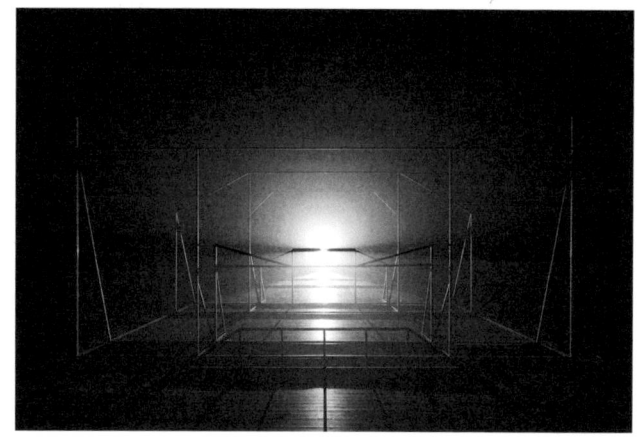

 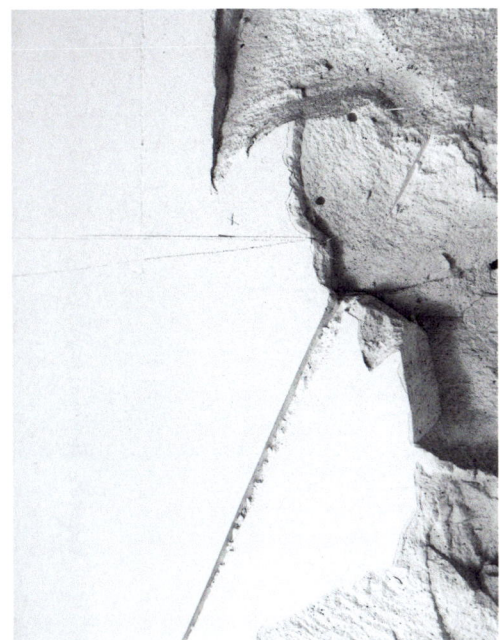

\+ I
ONE MORE SHORT STORY
BEFORE YOU GO
Daniel Zamarbide

In 2014 we participated in an exhibition at the Swiss Architecture Museum in Basel called *Orientations: Young Swiss Architects,* where, together with our colleague Sergey Ferley from Kiev, we presented the piece *MAIDAN*. The piece, a bit of a milestone for us, reflected on architecture's potential to be a politically engaged practice and a powerful tool to shape stories in public spheres, and so contained many layers, intuitions, representational tools, and attitudes that we would go on to pursue. The title of the exhibition was somehow very apropos for our work in the show: it pointed out an orientation.

Our office has evolved since. Ten years have passed, partners have changed as well. The A of Bureau A was dropped after a shift in partners in 2017 and we kept only Bureau, a rather absurd and generic name that could allow us to formulate and fabricate numerous things with an undetermined identity.

The initial premises that launched the office, we feel, have since prevailed, keeping us working along the same research lines and in the same territories. Most of our working time is taken up by exhibitions, displays, workshops, art-related contexts, residencies, magazines, objects, landscapes, renovations and a few newly built works. As much as we can, and despite the financial fragility that this type of practice often assumes, we continue to pursue this path, navigating among and along a variety of formats and mediums to stimulate spatial conditions and architecture.

We tend to arrange our work around two principal vectors: public space and domesticity. We like to call them vectors as they represent horizons of interest rather than enclosed categories or classifications. By public space we mean places and spaces that address to a wide possibility of free usage and practice, from temporary or permanent landscape and urban design to exhibitions where content and use are to be interpreted, experienced and debated at will, without a specific brief or agenda. Domesticity embraces everyday habitats and *habitus*, interiors, objects, houses, homes and everything that we are in close contact to support our daily routines and rituals. We acknowledge that much of the history of domesticity owes a great debt to the architecture produced and thought by women and female collectives. Another aspect that we have a growing interest in is cohabitation, in all its forms and with the inclusion of all living beings. There as well we feel the need to understand inhabitation and territorial occupation from a more-than-human perspective.

These two vectors have taken us to many places and encounters, to precious situations, and to locations, people and beings, all of which have shaped our thoughts and design. They have had us interacting with people and other species, with topics, issues, and histories, with fictional and nonfictional events and places. These exchanges are the constitutive parts of Bureaus stories. The work simply does not exist without this cascade of relationships.

One aspect of our work that this publication does not cover is pedagogy. Since the beginning of the Bureau, we have been involved in education in a variety of ways and places. This connection has nourished a lot of what we do. Mediation, transmission and intergenerational conversations are a very important part of our daily life.

This book presents some visual and textual stories of the practice's journeys, fragments of an always unfinished project that resists completion. Through our work and with the help of the texts in this publication, we have come to the conclusion that we don't need to see complete pieces of architecture to be stimulated and keep doing what we do. On the contrary, we are very excited about the many pieces that continue to evolve and might never provide "the," or "a" full picture. In this respect, the work of photographer Guido Guidi, which we saw recently, in August 2023, at the Canadian Centre for Architecture in Montreal, is inspirational. We feel very close to his way of relating to seemingly common situations through sequential and multiple points of view.

Short Stories unfolds our practice as a kaleidoscopic assemblage of projects that form our everyday life. There are no highlights for us. We get as excited by a yellow painted rectangle behind a Nuno Cera's picture in the *Distant Lights* exhibition at Sines, Portugal, as with the construction of a lighthouse in the Lake Geneva, Switzerland, which will turn its light on in spring 2025.

The textual stories have been very generously written by a wonderful set of creative individuals that have put their eyes and minds into our work, providing it an additional layer. We have been amazed by the variety of the proposals and the freedom of the writing.

Images are images and relate to a certain type of reality. The importance of photography for us is made evident in the manner in which our work is generally shown. We love photography and respect and fear its presence and power. This set of stories is very strongly marked by the strange and beautiful personality of the primary photographer of our work, Dylan Perrenoud, who has been carefully laying his intuitive eyes and mind on our work for a decade now.

The words and images presented here are completely intertwined with the physical work they refer to, the realized projects we have been making in the past years. We believe very strongly that all of these pieces—text, photography, and building—is part of the same construction, one that does not necessarily seek coherence but it is stimulated by hypothetical paths. It is as if, ten years ago, we started a long walk and continue to stumble upon new situations that modify our route. Ultimately, all of those encounters are the co-creators of what is shown here.

The whole is always less than
the sum of its parts
　　　—Timothy Morton

BUREAU TALKS

21-12-23 9:37 EST
14:37 GMT

AMIR HALABI and
AVA VIOLICH-KENNEDY,
in conversation with

CARINE PIMENTA,
DANIEL ZAMARBIDE,
and GALLIANE ZAMARBIDE

AMIR: We can begin by considering the word "bureau," which has roots in the seventeenth-century French word *burel*, meaning office desk or writing table, and by metonymy, has come to mean an office for collecting and distributing information. When describing your own practice, you use another definition of BUREAU: a practice that, under its generic name [gesticulates], hides a variety of research activities; a furniture series; an editorial project; and a design and architecture team. Can you reflect on what the term "bureau" means as an identity and as an attitude toward how each of you conceives of a creative practice today?

GALLIANE: In French-speaking parts of Switzerland, "bureau" means an architecture office. Sometimes when people talk about our practice in Switzerland, they're confused and say "bureau BUREAU" or "office office," which of course, is very strange [laughs, shifts in seat]. We love being introduced this way—it's exactly what we initially wanted.
DANIEL: The whole idea behind the name was to be generic somehow so as not to state that architecture had to be one thing. There's a little bit of intentional absurdity built in, as Galliane was saying. But there's a lot of indeterminacy built in that references many definitions and scales. [Pushes glasses up on nose.]
One is exactly what you mentioned, the desk—this very intimate crafted object for reading, writing, and introspecting. Then there's the larger institutional "bureau," which is cloudier—bringing to mind the FBI and organizations in more mysterious lines of work than architecture. So when we were thinking of the name originally, there was definitely a bit of that underlying it, too. And even though "BUREAU" might seem reductive, many years later, we still like it, I must say.

AVA: A generic name can bring about a productive line of questioning. It resists formalizing a definition of what a practice represents by allowing the name to hold less importance than the work and process behind it.

CARINE: Our definition of "BUREAU" really goes from space to furniture and even to people. BUREAU also includes our team, past and present. The name corresponds to the multiple scales of intervention that we work at, and in that sense, being very generic means exactly the opposite—it means being able to do many very specific things within or under one very simple name.
I really identify with it myself. But we do still get some resistance. Occasionally people refuse to call us just "BUREAU," and they insist on calling us, you know, "BUREAU A-C" or something, because of our website domain sequence. Some people really need a name!
DANIEL: Maybe our name sounded ridiculous from the start [laughs]. But simultaneously, being just BUREAU has given us so much freedom. We could have given the name a specifier, but we always wanted it to be an open box where you can put anything. Not just an architecture office—even though what we do is architecture, whether it's a desk or an object or a space-related intervention.

AMIR: BUREAU's projects span a wide range of scales and contexts. Is there any kind of intentionality when these projects come to conception or is the decision to take on something new rooted mainly in what feels exciting to you?

GALLIANE: We're not really dogmatic—we're open to everything.
DANIEL: There's a general habit in the office to be always cooking something up [laughs].
Most of the time, the projects are there before they're commissioned, if you know what I mean. We try to follow our interests all the time. We're not workaholics, but there's this underlying tendency that we share between the three of us that transforms anything that we see, feel, and experience into possible starting points for architecture. We're scanning for ideas constantly, whether we're reading a book or spending time with our families or going for a walk.
CARINE: The work we take on is really linked with natural curiosity. Sometimes we have ideas without having projects.
We've been working quite a lot with exhibition design and with renovations, and the existing sites in both these projects are a major source of inspiration. The smallest details that catch our eye are often the best starting places, in terms of potential of ideas or what we can bring or add to those spaces to transform them [leans inward, shoulders tense up].

AMIR: Mr. Barrett's House or the Dodged House come to mind—those projects deal with existing conditions but at the same time transform them. Could you speak about the practice's evolving process in terms of your relationships with place and materials?

CARINE: Mr. Barrett and the Dodged House are very different formally and materially and are also in two radically different contexts: Mr. Barrett's is in an open garden in Switzerland and the Dodged House is on a dense urban block in Lisbon. These different sites were crucial to the interventions we chose for each project and our attitudes towards what was there already. With the Dodged House, respecting the social and economic context of Lisbon was a major consideration, while with Mr. Barrett's House, we were more concerned with the existing building. But in each of the two projects, our strategy isn't so different—creating negative space was something we really valued in both cases. Even in a house as small as Mr. Barrett's, we allowed ourselves to create voids in the interior. It's really a statement of how much we value space in addition to other elements.
DANIEL: Mr. Barrett's House is actually the house of the caretaker of a much bigger house. We didn't even try to do the renovation of the mansion itself—we choose to intervene in the garden and what was basically a garage [laughs]. But the plot was very cool. We couldn't resist.
GALLIANE: We chose the garage—and we got it! [Laughs.]

— BREAK

AVA: BUREAU is led by the three of you. Could you reflect on what working as a trio has allowed you to achieve in terms of how the practice operates?

DANIEL: It's funny because three is kind of a notorious number for most organizations [smiles wryly].
GALLIANE: When you're three, you become a family. Having that kind of relationship is important, not only between the three of us but also with the office and the team.
DANIEL: A triangle is the strongest form in nature. Somehow, we're at the very minimum of what it takes to maintain stability. It's the fact that the three of us have different responsibilities, different attitudes, and different personalities that make the practice work so solidly. From the outside, it could seem like we're an office with fifteen employees because we're international and here and there. But the whole thing is so small. And we're always moving—we are hardly ever in one place together, which creates a very dynamic situation somehow, with each point always moving. [The three look at each other in agreement.]

AVA: A triangulation of floating points, more or less.

DANIEL: Exactly. Of course, we have our headquarters in Lisbon and Geneva, but it's as if the triangle's points are always readjusting towards where the others are. It's very important to present the office in this way, as a network between the three of us. There's a strong interpersonal aspect to it—there's a lot of trust between us, and that trust is the main core of our partnership. If tomorrow Carine wanted to do textiles, we would do textiles. If Galliane wanted to live in Chile, we'd go to Chile. In that sense, it's very simple. It's simpler than a real family, actually [laughs].

AMIR: There's also something to say about where the office is geographically located, between Geneva and Lisbon. Those two cities have very different characters. How do you reflect on the impact of working across these two very different cities?

DANIEL: When we're working at the Lisbon office, photographs from past teams and paper lobsters from the holiday party three years ago are still on the walls. Things aren't really polished, but that's a reflection of the environment around us—the office is just below a field full of roosters, so we couldn't be too corporate even if we tried [laughs].
The office is a representation of BUREAU, and in some ways holds a lot of our identity as a practice. It's our face. It's a place of work, but it's also a very social space where we host dinners and throw parties, and welcome people to the office and to the city. We designed it to be a space that can quickly transform to be able to host all kinds of events. We also have different fragments of former projects and installations—we have *"THE CLUB"* and the *"MONTE VERITA"* fountain in the middle of the office.
GALLIANE: The Lisbon office has a way of bringing things and people together. But the Geneva office has its special qualities too. Our office there is in an industrial area where there are a lot of craftsmen and artisans. It's a very specific feature of the Geneva construction landscape and it's been an influence on our work too.

AMIR: Here's a scene from my memories in Lisbon. You have that long table that's always scattered with hand sketches, printed screenshots, coffee grinds, and random things that don't relate to one another. Carine is jumping between tasks, Galliane is red-lining and lurking around, and Daniel is pacing the room talking about films I have never heard of. It's constant conversation where references from cinema, architecture, and history are flying in left and right. How did you arrive at that kind of a working atmosphere?

DANIEL: Things definitely move more efficiently now than in the early days of the office, but the freedom in our working style is even stronger today. After many years of working together our trust in one another has only deepened. We're a very unexpected trio—we don't come from the same schools, we didn't start together, we don't even come from the same countries or backgrounds. All of this has forced us to be even more open with one another, somehow.
CARINE: Galliane's background is in social studies and also in photography, which is an important complement to what the office does and perceives itself as. Daniel and I are trained as architects, but at one point, we began using the term spatial practitioners. I'm comfortable being an architect, but it's not a title I need.
DANIEL: I come from a middle-class family that wasn't interested in contemporary art or architecture in any way. That's a part of our origins too. We look at culture in a relatively simple way, with an open curiosity to what is usually called popular culture as much as any other "type" of culture. Is this distinction really necessary, useful? Daft Punk is cool! [Laughs.] In that sense, the three of us also understand each other quite well. There's no pedantic attitude towards our profession or ourselves.

— BREAK

AMIR: Time is an important aspect of BUREAU's work. It always seems as though your current projects draw in elements from the history of visual arts and media through film, photography, image composition, and so on. Could you reflect on how you view the past, present, and future in your work?

CARINE: Things like materials and construction and the act of building somehow are both present and future, especially in some of our most recent projects. We've been talking a lot about the environmental impacts of the project we propose. In that sense, even with practical matters in the present, there's a sense of looking toward the future.

DANIEL: Something that has stayed with me since my studies is the naïve trace of something that many architects have that leads you to want to change the world, even if only a little bit. As stupid as it may sound, I think that stays with me still today [gazes outward reflectively]. You could call that the utopian nature of the profession—when you try to provoke questioning or change through your work. We always try to change things through design that we don't agree with, or that we feel are unfair. This is shared between the three of us. Once I started putting my feet deeper into the art world, I realized the existential questioning wasn't so much a concern for me. We don't need to leave traces behind to signal we were there. Once a building is done, it's done, and we don't care so much whether in a hundred years somebody says this was done by BUREAU. The future isn't about that. That's also why we like exhibition design so much, maybe even more than conventional architecture. Exhibitions are very public, and you get to work much more in the present to try to change, somehow, a certain aspect of how people perceive culture. When you go to see an exhibition, you find yourself in a space that was designed to encourage you to reflect. There isn't the goal of permanence, of designing something that will remain there forever [nods head back slightly, adjusts posture]. Galliane and I are living in Quebec at the moment, and one of the things we've come to appreciate about time is really how you use it. In our collaborations as an office, time is extremely precious. I've never felt any pressure from Carine and Galliane about how we spend the time that we have. Sometimes, good ideas take time. We can be slow in thinking one day and leave ourselves a lot of time for something the next. For me, that's one of the jewels of our office—the fact that we can give ourselves that time.

CARINE: Related to time but also to the idea of pacing and schedules is the fact that when you work across the scales of exhibition design, competitions, housing projects, etcetera, each consumes a very different amount of time. An exhibition design we'll maybe do within four months, and in parallel, we'll do a house that takes two or three years, and in between a competition in eight weeks. This diversity isn't unique to our office, but for me it's a part of thinking of the present and future as well—the timing of different projects and how they overlap brings a constant dynamism to our work.

DANIEL: The idea of chronology is something interesting in our profession. Why do things have to be chronological? All our projects are still with us, somehow. One of the things we've been discussing between the three of us is going back to some of our older projects, ones that have been built for a while already, and taking new photographs. We've been trying to deconstruct conventional project phasing a lot lately. We don't think of phasing as a three-step process of concept development, detailing, and construction. For us, once you hand in a project, it's not just gone. It still exists in relation to our other works, past, present, and future. The photographs and structuring of the monograph reflect this chronological mix of associations and juxtapositions. We think about our work and projects across time, and those relationships change with time too. The creative process isn't linear. Just because you have one idea or see in one way today doesn't mean it sticks with you forever. There's a constant looping of how projects connect to one another, and how we look at them as well.

GALLIANE: The projects in the monograph aren't in a chronological sequence, but that somehow feels accurate to how we work and live. We start with the design of a house and deliver the project three years later. During that time, we may have already finished four, six, even ten other projects that all began after the start of the house. The monograph is about short stories, much like the ones we live through in our lives. Our projects overlap all the time, as our three lives do. The work, practice, and process of the office is relayed through multiple stories that intertwine and take place simultaneously. We tried to relay that through the monograph's structure. It's a visual story you enter. You look around, see something that catches your eye, and then you can piece connections together between projects that exist individually but also all at once, somehow.

AMIR: In the monograph, photography allows you to speak about relationality — between what you design and its context, but between two photographs on the page too. There are traces that run throughout the book, like Chekhov's gun. In a way, the narrative of the monograph unfolds through these recurring visual themes rather than through any kind of chronological ordering.

DANIEL: Another part of that relationality includes our own connections with the people we work with — in the case of the monograph, Dylan Perrenoud and Fábio Cunha, with whom we have a special relationship, for photography and Manuel Krebs from NORM for graphic design.

CARINE: We choose who we work with, but not what they do, in the end. There's a lot of trust there. We believe in multiple ways of seeing and in a very free process of collaboration, which is maybe not so common.

GALLIANE: We wanted them to have a carte blanche. Of course, that doesn't mean that there's no dialogue. We spent quite some time with Manu in Zürich for the graphic design of the book, working back and forth. But we had total trust in him.

DANIEL: Somehow, it goes back to our earlier discussion about the name of the office — once you have a practice that fits within it so much trust, things happen naturally. What Carine said is very important. We choose who we work with because they have competencies, but the basis of our choice is really on the person themselves. We work with great people–people we really like. Having that basis for the relationship opens new opportunities that influence us too and allow us to look at our work differently.

GALLIANE: And people who know us very well too. For example, I've known Dylan since I was a teenager and he's also a very old friend of Daniel's. The kind of understanding we share is something we've built over many years.

DANIEL: When you look at the monograph, everything feels very coherent. It's surprising, somehow, because of course every project introduces us to new people and new teams who bring things to the table that take the work and direction of the office to different places. To have coherence at the end of the day speaks to a shared set of values.

CARINE: We're not an office that repeats projects. There is a certain visual coherence that Dylan's talent as photographer gives to the work, but it's not coherence by repetition. We do share some elements across different projects in terms of materials, attitudes, or colour palette, but the coherence really develops in how we think about the work itself. The aspect that's more important is space and how space is perceived, whether that's in an exhibition design or in a house.

GALLIANE: Maybe it's the same voids that appear in the monograph. White space is also an important feature in the book—it's a kind of void too, in a way. You need that emptiness on the page to really understand and draw connections between the images.

DANIEL: Space and time—we're getting very Heideggerian now [laughs].

GALLIANE: But coherence is also the result of a long process of dialogue and reflection on the representation of our work.

DANIEL: We consider the representation of the work we do as part of the work itself. It relates to the question of what constitutes architecture. Are drawings architecture? Is photography architecture? We believe in the importance of photography and image in general. Photography in the traditional sense is represented in the office by Galliane, but we take interest in images of all kinds and that comes through art as well.

AVA: Each project is represented as a collection of photographs of details and fragments that comprise a whole. In a way, it seems like a mirror of how you see your practice too.

DANIEL: Our work is exactly that—a multiplicity of fragments. It's fragments of Lisbon, fragments of Switzerland, fragments of Quebec these days, fragments of the people that we meet—and all of these fragments are somehow floating in time and space. They don't need to be synthesized. The monograph is a bit like that. You don't have a clear image of what the projects are, or what BUREAU is, in the end. But you don't need that either. It doesn't exist. The office exists in different times and cities. It's an assemblage of fragments that are all linked—an insight into our minds.

INDEX

AFR
A-Frame
– Installation piece for the Triennale du Valais 2017
A landscape piece in dialogue with a specific site and history of American A-frame and catalogue constructions.
– Steel structure on floating barrels, mirror polished stainless steel, neon
– 2017, Martigny, Switzerland
Photography Dylan Perrenoud

AG1
Antigel Festival
– Temporary club (Le Grand Central) for music and other live performances
– Re-use materials and objects, neon lights / 400 m²
– 2015, Geneva, Switzerland
Photography Dylan Perrenoud
With Leopold Banchini architects

AG2
Antigel Festival
– Scenography and club (Le Grand Central) within an existing factory in phase of demolition
– Re-use materials, demolition, paint / 2000 m²
– 2016, Geneva, Switzerland
Photography Dylan Perrenoud
With Leopold Banchini architects

ALA
Alamp 5421
– A furniture light piece
A tribute to Achille Castiglioni's 1954 Luminator lamp.
– Welded solid metal, thermo-painted in three colours
– 2021
Photography Fábio Cunha

ANT
Antoine
– An inhabitable sculpture in the Swiss Alps for the 3D foundation art residency and sculpture park
Looking to bunker architecture and the impossible (or very difficult) idea of making nature-like architectures.
– Three-ply hardwood panels, metal bars and bolts, shotcrete on metal mesh and hard foam insulation / 4 m²
– 2014, Swiss Alps over Verbier, Switzerland
Photography Dylan Perrenoud
With Leopold Banchini architects

AST
L'Asticot
– Interior design for children concept Store L'Asticot
– Metal furniture, cardboard model, neon lights / 30 m²
– 2014, Geneva, Switzerland
Photography Dylan Perrenoud
With Leopold Banchini architects

BAG
Mr. Barrett's Garden
– Garden design for a large suburban property
A poetic and picturesque approach to garden design.
– Structural metal beams, Ipe wooden platforms, Oregon pine wood sauna structure, reclaimed stone and concrete furniture, native meadow vegetation, flowered lawn, fruit tree, oak tree, beech tree, birch tree, shrubs and climber plants / 5000 m²
– 2020, Genthod, Switzerland
Photography Dylan Perrenoud

BAH
Mr. Barrett's House
– Transformation of an old garage and small apartment into a house
A full wood construction within the existing architecture. Creating interior voids and perceptual richness for everyday life.
– Wood structure, plywood birch panels, micro-cement / 70 m²
– 2019, Genthod, Switzerland
Photography Dylan Perrenoud

BAS
Base Design Geneva Headquarters
– Workspace design to host the graphic design studio of BASE Geneva
A multifunctional bleacher hosting all functions: working, informal sitting, events and exhibitions.
– Standard section wood lumbers, standard cement slabs / 340 m²
– 2013, Geneva, Switzerland
Photography Régis Golay (Federal)
With Leopold Banchini architects

BBB
BBB
– Transformation of a sandwich shop
Furniture design
Dealing with a small and intricate space to turn it into a special family restaurant.
– Concrete table piece poured into stainless steel structure, thermo-painted metal and birch plywood furniture and metal light fixture / 44 m²
– 2020, Lisbon, Portugal
Photography Dylan Perrenoud

BEY
Beyond the Monument
– Exhibition design for a group research project by the University of Art and Design HEAD – Genève at Le Commun art space
Giving research in an exhibition status through the presentation of texts as much as artworks.
– Curated by Denis Pernet
– Solid metal rods, concrete supports, printed paper / 450 m²
– 2015, Geneva, Switzerland, Photography Bureau A
With Leopold Banchini architects

BG1
BIG15
– Masterplan and display for the Independent Art Spaces Biennale of Geneva
Urban composition allowing flexibility of uses and creating gathering.
– Maritime containers / 1750 m²
– 2015, Geneva, Switzerland
Photography Dylan Perrenoud
With Leopold Banchini architects

BG2
BIG17
– Masterplan and display for the Independent Art Spaces Biennale of Geneva
Urban composition allowing flexibility of uses and creating gathering.
– Maritime containers / 3000 m²
– 2017, Geneva, Switzerland
Photography Dylan Perrenoud

BIN
Bada Bing Boardwalk
– Master planning of the boardwalk and event space for the Montreux Jazz Festival
Temporary platforms on water with a sequence of specific gates with new neon pop identities.
– Metal arches on "panettone"-shaped concrete supports, bespoke neon lights, wooden library shelving with DJ booth / 435 m²
– 2013, Montreux, Switzerland
Photography Dylan Perrenoud
With Leopold Banchini architects

BOU
Bout
– Useless and multipurpose marble object
After a study of Paleolithic stone tools.
– 2017
Photography Fábio Cunha

BUR
The BUREAU
– Transformation of a warehouse into a flexible atelier space
Furniture design
Minimal intervention respecting the memory and history of the place.
– Estremoz pink marble slabs, thermo-painted metal supports

and furniture pieces, paint / 180 m²
- 2020, Lisbon, Portugal
Photography Dylan Perrenoud

CCS
Centre Culturel Suisse Paris
- Semi-temporary transformation of existing space for the thirtieth anniversary of the CCSP
Creation of a new open space with atmospheric wood structure and a generic performance neutral space for exhibitions and performative events.
- Wood vertical beams, vinyl flooring, mobile furniture and technical pieces, screens, bespoke neon lights / 280 m²
- 2015, Paris, France
Photography Dylan Perrenoud
With Leopold Banchini architects

CDM
Casa do Monte
- New house on Lisbon top hill
- Concrete, Estremoz pink and white marble, thermo-painted solid metal furniture, cork / 200 m²
- 2019, Lisbon, Portugal
Photography Dylan Perrenoud
With Leopold Banchini architects

CIR
Le Cercle
- Temporary fair space and furniture for Le Cercle, an association of independent editors and publishers
A series of minimal kiosks constructed of metal lines with bespoke neon signs.
- Thermo-painted metal frames and furniture, painted three-ply hardwood panels, neon light tubes, tyvek curtain / 490 m²
- 2016–2020, Geneva, Switzerland
Photography Dylan Perrenoud
With Leopold Banchini architects

DIN
Lake Diner
- A temporary bar and shelter structure for one outdoor venue of the Montreux Jazz Festival
An interpretation of the magic of the American diners.
- Steel and stainless-steel structure, mirror polished stainless steel, neon and light bulbs / 350 m²
- 2016, Montreux, Switzerland
Photography Dylan Perrenoud
With Leopold Banchini architects

DIR
Direktor
- Stage design for the theatre company l'Alakran (Oscar Gómez Mata)
A referential and spatial background that echoes Oskar Schlemmer's Triadic ballet—and hosts a quite wild crew.

- Steel structure, printed vinyl
Stage dimension / 100 m²
- 2017, Geneva, Switzerland and itinerant
Photography Dylan Perrenoud

DOG
Dodged House
- Transformation of a dense urban site to host a new house
Space making within a small plot. Stacked programs, space, voids, views and multiple layers versus square meters.
- Standard cement blocks, glass, pivot rounded window, sanded concrete, standard tiles, Estremoz marble pieces, thermo-painted solid metal furniture and stairs / 94 m²
- 2019, Lisbon, Portugal
Photography Dylan Perrenoud
With Leopold Banchini architects

EAU
Spirulina Fountain
- A temporary landscape-design intervention for Villes et Champs landscape festival
A free reenactment of the sixteenth century villa Aldobrandini fountain in Italy turning it into an instrument for producing spirulina.
- Plywood, spirulina algae, water 100 m long fountain / 75 m²
- 2014, Geneva, Switzerland
Photography Dylan Perrenoud
With Leopold Banchini architects

FAB
Fabrique de Jardin
- A garden pavilion made out of reclaimed windows / 14 m²
- 2013, Geneva, Switzerland
Photography
David Gagnebin-de Bons
With Leopold Banchini architects

FLO
Floating Realities
- Transformation of a health and well-being space for saltwater floating experience.
An attempt to work with color surfaces, sequences and space as the main characters of the intervention.
- Semi-handmade tiles, paint, bespoke thermo-painted solid metal furniture, textile curtains / 190 m²
- 2020, Geneva, Switzerland
Photography Dylan Perrenoud

FLY
Bird Shelter
- A shelter in an animal park to protect Anatidae from being polluted by migrant flying birds (avian influenza periods – H5N1)
A landscaped shelter with sixteen tree-like metal pillars camouflaged in a picturesque context.
- Thermo-painted structural steel tubes, stainless-steel mesh, concrete slab poured onsite 9-meter high roof and pillars / 300 m²
- 2008, Geneva, Switzerland
Photography Dylan Perrenoud
With group8 architects

FNT
Fountain 2017
- A fountain and public urinal for the exhibition and settlement Common Ground
- Marble slab, copper pipes, wooden structure, plants / 10 m²
- 2015, Zurich, Switzerland
Photography James Batten
Bureau A
With Leopold Banchini architects

GOS
Ghost Drop
- Art and architecture research residency for Matza Collective project
An installation piece in the desert transforming evaporated water into drinkable water.
- Glued glass pyramid, windmill, on site poured-concrete bench
- 2016, Amboy, California, USA
Photography Galliane Zamarbide
Maxime Bondu
With Maxime Bondu and Leopold Banchini architects

JAK
Jack Bar
- A temporary bar on the roof of an iconic alternative venue in Geneva: l'Usine
- Scaffolding tubes, earth bags, neon light and plants
- 2012, Geneva, Switzerland
Photography Dylan Perrenoud
With Guillaume Yersin architect and Leopold Banchini architects

KLB
The Club
- A series of event around historical places in the Lisbon area for the Lisbon Architecture Triennale 2016
Designed and built architectural sound system that has travelled over the diverse sites and elsewhere around the world.
- Agglomerated wood, loudspeaker components / 11 m²
- 2016, Lisbon area, Portugal and itinerant
Photography Dylan Perrenoud
Mariana Lopes
With Leopold Banchini architects

LAM
Lampedusa
- Stage design for theatre company Souschiffre (Dorothée Thébert-

234

Filliger and Filippo Filliger) for the performance "Lampedusa, un rocher de survie"
A series of design and architectural objects creating spatial situations while interacting with the comedians and storytellers.
– Solid metal pink thermo-painted poles, leather gloves, earth mound, LED light strips
Stage dimension / 100 m²
– 2019, Geneva, Switzerland
Photography Dylan Perrenoud

L7G
7G
– Display for the theater play "La 7G" of Sébastien Grosset
– Suspended glass panels, film
– 2022, different theater venues, Switzerland
Photography Dylan Perrenoud

LAU
Laura
– A piece of furniture for multiple uses.
– Estremoz pink marble
– 2023
Photography Fábio Cunha

MAI
Maidan
– Exhibition piece for Orientations Young Swiss Architects at Swiss Architecture Museum (SAM) in Basel
Installation on the capacity of temporary works and objects to produce intelligent architecture.
– Reenacted stainless-steel shields, massive wood joints, video
– 2014, Basel, Switzerland and itinerant
Photography Bureau A
With Sergey Ferley architect and Leopold Banchini architects

MAM
Maison Molaire
– Transformation of a dentist office into a domestic flexible space
Working outside the notion of typology and accepting the flux of life in any inhabitation.
– Standard wood industrial panels, glass, felt and polyethylene curtains, handmade tiles, bespoke metal furniture / 120 m²
– 2022–23, Geneva, Switzerland
Photography Dylan Perrenoud

MAR
Maria
– Transformation of a living space in Anjos, Lisbon
Working on spaces that try to question the nuclear family dominating typology.
– Structural metal beams, Estremoz marble, handmade tiles, glass, blackout curtains / 90 m²

– 2020, Lisbon, Portugal
Photography Francisco Nogueira

MIG
Migrant Gardens
– Design of an object for Migrant Gardens, Untouchable landscapes
– Perforated glass, organic earth, metal and living worm
25 × 25 cm
– 2015, Politecnico di Milano, Piacenza, Italy
Photography Bureau A
With Leopold Banchini architects

MOB
Mobile Republic
– Three mobile pieces for the festival Abandon Normal Devices in Manchester and Liverpool
A micro-cinema, a micro art space and a gathering wood tent.
– Reclaimed and transformed trailers, upholstery, standard wood joists
Various trailers / 4 m²
– 2014, Manchester, Liverpool, UK
Photography Régis Golay (Federal)
With Leopold Banchini architects

MON
Monte Verità
– A set design for the Arc en Rêve exhibition *Constellations*
A photographic and research project on the Swiss utopian community of Monte Verità.
– Solid metal fountain structure and furniture, sculpted marble piece, 3D-printed miniatures
– 2016, Bordeaux, France
Photography Dylan Perrenoud
Fábio Cunha
Bureau A
With Leopold Banchini architects

MUR
Mush Rooms
– Set design and performance for Critical Cooking Show at the MAAT Museum
A performance and film for the fifth Istanbul Design Biennial *Empathy Revisited: Designs for More than One.*
Cooking, architecture, design, performance and sound around a text by anthropologist Anna Tsing.
With chef Walter El Nagar and sound artist Filipe Felizardo
Curated by Mariana Pestana with Sumitra Upham and Billie Muraben
– Plastic tent suspended to thermo-painted cylinder metal beam, Estremoz marble leftovers pieces from quarry / 200 m²
– 2020, Lisbon, Portugal, Istanbul, Turkey
Photography Francisco Craveiro Santos

NUN
Distant Lights
– Exhibition design for a retrospective show on photographer and video artist Nuno Cera at the Center of Arts of Sines
A landscape of possibilities to experience Nuno Cera's images through a very simple and spatial approach.
Curated by Julia Albani and José Mouro
– Paint, reclaimed pedestals / 1150 m²
– 2022, Sines, Portugal
Photography Nuno Cera

OAK
7000 Oaks
– Public spaces around one of the new CEVA train stations
Creating a tree milieu by planting a maximum of oak trees in an urban fabric.
– Diversity of oak trees, fiber concrete prefabricated curved borders, bespoke benches and urban furniture, public lighting system / 15000 m²
– 2020, Geneva, Switzerland
Photography Dylan Perrenoud
Guillaume Collignon
With Leopold Banchini architects

PAN
Panorama Suburbia
– House extension and transformation
A material approach to the extension of a conventional modern house by the Lake Geneva.
– Natural wood plank formwork, concrete, black Ruivina marble slabs, cherry wood panels, curved glass / 50 m²
– 2016, Geneva, Switzerland
Photography Galliane Zamarbide
Dylan Perrenoud
With Leopold Banchini architects

PAR
Parole
– Installation for the Swiss Art Awards price in Basel
A research project on Geneva prison conditions using an architectural model as a sculpture.
– Self-welded metal frame, pamphlet
– 2013, Basel, Switzerland
Photography Dylan Perrenoud
With Leopold Banchini architects

POR
Portal
– Ornamental gate
– 10 mm thick laser cut metal plate
– 2012, Geneva, Switzerland
Photography Régis Golay (Federal)
With Leopold Banchini architects

ROG
Rigorism
– Stage design for the theatre company Allerlei (Marie Brillant) An approach to understand Serlio's scenes through a play of perspective and pop collage.
– Metal frames, printed large format collages
Stage dimension / 100 m²
– 2014, Grenoble, France
Photography Dylan Perrenoud
With Leopold Banchini architects

SAW
Sawerdo
– Transformation of an abandoned restaurant into a bakery and brunch space
A collective important table piece acts as a centrifugal relationship force.
– Estremoz pink marble, stainless steel, handmade tiles / 200 m²
– 2021, Geneva, Switzerland
Photography Dylan Perrenoud

SEL
Selenite Dreams
– Exhibition Design for the Audemars Piguet Musée Atelier Transformation Matière. An exhibition on how contemporary artists deal with the alterations of matter.
Curated by Denis Pernet
– Hand applied plaster on metal structure and mesh, handmade printed ceramic tiles / 24 m²
– 2022, Le Brassus, Switzerland
Photography Dylan Perrenoud

SFG
Scape from Germany
– Installation at M:AI – Museum für Architektur und Ingenieurkunst for a collective exhibition
– Large glass suspended table, earth, cactus, mirrors / 6 m²
– 2015, Gelsenkirchen, Germany
Photography Bureau A
With Leopold Banchini architects

SHE
Shelter
– An inflatable temporary club Following a study of buried architectures, a literal translation of a found typology.
– Inflatable pvc fabric membrane / 40 m²
– 2016, Geneva, Switzerland and itinerant
Photography Dylan Perrenoud
With Leopold Banchini architects

SWS
SwissNex
– Stage design for the opening of the SwissNex and Swiss embassy in San Francisco
– A playful series of soft furniture made out of recycled foam / 440 m²
– 2016, San Francisco, California, USA
Photography Dylan Perrenoud
With Leopold Banchini architects

TAB
BUREAU table
– Furniture design
– Semi-handmade tiles, thermo-painted solid metal structure
280 x 80 cm
– 2017
Photography Dylan Perrenoud

THE
Thérèse
– Intervention on the site of Bermuda Ateliers artists collective Les Bâtisseurs art and architecture, Seulgi Lee, Les Frères Chapuisat, Simon Boudvin and BUREAU.
An independent micro-inhabitation, an "habitacle"
Curated by Maxime Bondu, Mathilde Chénin, Bénédicte Le Pimpec and Guillaume Robert
– Wood industrial panels, reclaimed wood fiber insulation, shotcrete on metal mesh / 9 m²
– 2022, Sergy, France
Photography Dylan Perrenoud

TOM
Thomas Bar
– An installation as an inhabited alembic production device
Wood lumber and alembic
– 2012, Martigny, Switzerland
Photography Bureau A
With Leopold Banchini architects

TRI
Atricc Table
– A fragile piece to support a variety of things
– Acrylic colored rod, thermo-painted metal top
– 2017
Photography Fábio Cunha

VER
Monte Verità
– Stage design for theatre company Souschiffre (Dorothée Thébert-Filliger and Filippo Filliger)
A mobile wooden settlement to perform the play outdoors.
– Water tank, sauna, mobile furniture, stage and enclosures. Standard section wood joists, felt, bespoke neon lights
– 2014, Geneva, Switzerland and itinerant
Photography Dorothée Thébert-Filliger
With Leopold Banchini architects

VIS
Visionaries
– Exhibition design for the Lisbon Architecture Triennale 2022 at Culturgest Arts Center
An exhibition about visionary creative processes and alternative views of authorship.
A special focus on Dom Hans Van der Laan, Roger Anger and Anupama Kundoo.
Curated by Anastassia Smirnova
– Blackout curtains, paint, neon light sign / 685 m²
– 2022, Lisbon, Portugal
Photography Francisco Nogueira

WAN
Wwan Stool
– Different-height stools designed for BBB
Low, medium and high sitting
– Thermo-painted metal, birch plywood
– 2020, Lisbon, Portugal
Photography Fábio Cunha

XIN
X is not a Small Country
– Exhibition Design for the MAAT Museum
An exhibition that explores our current post-global condition by observing the processes of de-globalization and geopolitical realignment at different scales.
Curated by Aric Chen with Martina Muzi
– Adhesive tape, thermo-painted solid metal poles and furniture / 1921 m²
– 2021, Lisbon, Portugal
Photography Francisco Nogueira

BUREAU

Collaborators
2012–2024

Alain Van Garderen
Allegra Zanirato
Amir Halabi
Andrea Perletti
Andrea Tamm
Andreína Mosquera
Angelo Renna
Anna Scorretti
Caterina Spadoni
Charlotte Day
Chiara Pezzetta
Driss Veyry
Eleni Charcharidou
Erica Ubbiali
Flavio Gorgone
Francesco Lupia
Francisco Castelo Branco
Frederico Duarte Ferreira
Géraldine Singy
Giuseppe Semeraro
Gonçalo Frias
Hana Turnovská
Ignacio Martínez Pendás
Inès Acito
Inês Nunes
Ioannis Solis
Jeremy Morris
Joana Croft Dantas
Joana Duarte
João Paixão
Joël Berger
Jolan Haidinger
José Amorim
Juliette Roduit
Katerina Gkimizoudi
Laetitia Chauveau
Léo Raphaël
Leo Yuan
Lilian Pala
Lisa Brugière
Loïs Weber
Luísa Pires
Lujza Lehocká
Malak Abdelhady
Manuel La Casta Miras
Marco Pallaoro
María Sánchez
Marina Rondini
Martin Wecke
Matilde Mozzi
Mélanie Ganino
Merilin Kaup
Miguel Gomes
Myriam Marti
Natalia Juan
Noémie Girardet
Pauline Tondreau
Pedro Saraiva
Peter Bauer
Pierre Musy
Robinson Mangematin
Rui Da Silva
Taïma Matthes
Tanja Reichmuth
Thibault Pierron
Tobias Vonder Mühll
Todor Rusev
Valentin Racine
Vanessa Pointet
Veera Gontsugova
Victoria Alvarez Calvo
Vivien Manuel
William Jaulain

BUREAU

Bureau is the research-oriented practice of DANIEL ZAMARBIDE, CARINE PIMENTA and GALLIANE ZAMARBIDE. The office concentrates its work on three main vectors: domesticity, public space and pedagogy.

The creative and singular approach of the practice was nominated for the Mies van der Rohe Award 2022, won the Prix de Genève 2021, the Gold and Blue Award Best Architect 22 Germany, the Swiss Design Awards in 2019, the Swiss Art Awards, the Prix Design Suisse with the ALICE-EPFL laboratory, and the Frame Awards, among many others.

DANIEL graduated from the IAUG (Institut d'Architecture Université de Genève) and has been very influenced by art since his studies. He co-founded group8 architects in Geneva, Switzerland, and Hanoi, Vietnam, in 2000, which he left in 2012. He has taught and developed progressive pedagogical programs mainly at HEAD-Geneva, University of Laval in Canada and EPFL Lausanne as co-director of ALICE. His current practice – BUREAU – was initially formed in 2012 with Leopold Banchini (then called BUREAU A) and changed partners in 2017.

CARINE graduated from FAUP (Faculdade de Arquitectura da Universidade do Porto) and attended the EPFL (École Polytechnique Fédérale de Lausanne). She developed a particular sensitivity to a socially engaged approach of architecture which led her to work for ateliermob. Her interests lie in participatory and inclusive processes. Her knowledge and experience cover the technicalities of construction detailing and site supervision. She worked during 4 years for the BUREAU before becoming a partner in 2019.

GALLIANE graduated from the visual communication department at ECAL (Ecole Cantonale d'Art de Lausanne), with a specialization in photography. She became a partner of the BUREAU in 2017 bringing to the practice a different orientation and openness to design, image and installation projects. She works as the head of fine arts department for primary school state pedagogy in Geneva. She is currently teaching at the HEAD-Geneva master (MAIA).

AUTHORS

AMIR HALABI is a designer trained in architecture at Texas Tech University and the Harvard Graduate School of Design. With a long-standing interest in scenography he has worked with several cultural institutions, including exhibition designs and curatorial projects at MAAT, the Beirut Art Center, and the Harvard Art Museums. He is also a former team member of BUREAU.

FABRIZIO GALLANTI is a curator and architect with international experience in architectural design, education, and in making publications and exhibitions. He is the founding partner of the research studio FIG Projects, established in 2003, and has been the director of arc en rêve – centre d'architecture, in Bordeaux, since 2021.

ZACCHARIE LACHANCE is a farmer and architect based in Charlevoix, Québec.

ALEXANDRA MIDAL is an independent curator and professor at the University of Art and Design HEAD – Genève (HES-SO) and Head of the Department of Critical Thinking at Ensci—Les Ateliers in Paris. A distinguished historian of art and design, she combines practice and theory-based research as an artist-curator, theoretician, and film essayist. Her research explores the blind spots and grey areas of design history, as evident in her two latest books, *The Murder Factory* (Sternberg Press, 2023) and *Design by Accident: For a New History of Design* (Sternberg Press, 2019). Midal studied literature, architecture, and art history at Princeton University and in Paris, completing her doctoral thesis at Paris Sorbonne while a Rome Prize recipient in architecture at Villa Medici. She has curated a number of international exhibitions about visual culture, design and politics, such as Double Agent: Do You Speak Flower? (Design Biennial, Ljubljana, 2024–5), *Top Secret: Cinema and Espionage, Politique Fiction*, and *Tomorrow Now—When Design Meets Science*. Her films, including *Mind's Eyes*, *Possessed*, *Heaven is a State of Mind*, have been screened in museums across the globe.

DR. MARINA OTERO VERZIER is an architect and researcher currently teaching at Columbia University's Graduate School of Architecture, Planning, and Preservation. In 2022, she received Harvard's Wheelwright Prize. Previously, she was Head of the MA Social Design at Design Academy Eindhoven (2020–23), Director of Research at Het Nieuwe Instituut (2015–22), and Director of Global Programming at Studio-X (2013–15).

ANDRÉ TAVARES is a researcher at the Faculty of Architecture of the University of Porto, founding director of Dafne Editora and the author of *The Anatomy of the Architectural Book* (Lars Müller/CCA, 2016) and *Vitruvius Without Text* (gta Verlag, 2022). His current research, Fishing Architecture, is funded by the European Research Council.

AVA VIOLICH-KENNEDY is a designer and researcher based in Boston, USA. Ava received her undergraduate degree in History and Literature from Harvard College and her graduate degree in architecture with distinction from the Harvard Graduate School of Design. Her current work is interested in architecture's relationship with coastal ecologies, infrastructures, and communities, most recently in the parish of Terrebonne in southern Louisiana.

TIRDAD ZOLGHADR has worked as a curator, writer and arts educator since 2003. Published writing includes fiction, art criticism and curatorial research, e.g. *REALTY: Beyond the Traditional Blueprints of Art & Gentrification* (Hatje Cantz Berlin, 2022). Curating includes biennial settings as well as long-term collective initiatives. Most recently Zolghadr was Guest Professor at the postgraduate program of the University of the Arts Berlin. Since 2012 he has been a regular advisor at the Rijksakademie van beeldende Kunsten Amsterdam.

SHORT STORIES
PIECES OF ARCHITECTURE

Editors:
Daniel Zamarbide
Galliane Zamarbide
Carine Pimenta

Copyediting and proofreading:
Andrew Scheinman
Translations from French:
Daniel Zamarbide

Design: NORM, Zurich
Photography: Dylan Perrenoud
(unless otherwise mentioned)

Printing and binding:
DZA Druckerei zu Altenburg
Paper: Werkdruck 15
Typeface: Univers LT

ISBN 978-3-03860-373-3

© 2025 Bureau, the authors and photographers
www.bureau.ac

All rights reserved. No part of this publication may be reproduced in any form or by any electronic or mechanical means (including photocopying, recording, or information storage and retrieval systems) without permission in writing from the publishers. Every effort has been made to trace copyright ownership and to obtain reproduction permissions. Corrections brought to the publisher's attention will be incorporated in future reprints or editions of this book.

Park Books
Niederdorfstrasse 54
8001 Zürich
www.park-books.com

Park Books is being supported by the Federal Office of Culture with a general subsidy for the years 2021–2025.

With the support of the Swiss Arts Council Pro Helvetia

prohelvetia